Exercising Your Authority over Fear

Exercising Your Authority over Fear

† A Manual for Christians †

Jane E. Eke

iUniverse, Inc.
Bloomington

Exercising Your Authority over Fear
A Manual for Christians

iUniverse books may be ordered through booksellers or by contacting:

iUniverse
1663 Liberty Drive
Bloomington, IN 47403
www.iuniverse.com
1-800-Authors (1-800-288-4677)

ISBN: 978-1-4759-5578-1 (sc)
ISBN: 978-1-4759-5577-4 (hc)
ISBN: 978-1-4759-5576-7 (e)

Library of Congress Control Number: 2012919323

Printed in the United States of America

iUniverse rev. date: 10/18/2012

Table of Contents

Dedication

Special thanks go to my Lord Jesus Christ, who is my inspiration, instructor and the originator of this book - for without Him, I am nothing.

To my parents and siblings, I want to thank you for your unfailing love, care and support. I bless God for your lives and thank you for supporting the vision and calling of God for my life. Thank you for standing by me at all times and may the good Lord bless you and reward you more abundantly.

Finally, I dedicate this book to the Body of Christ especially those who have allowed fear to gripped their hearts and minds as well as snatch their great destiny in God. This book is designed to help you understand the consequences of fear, how it separate you from God, how to stand your ground and exercise your authority in Christ.

Acknowledgement

My special thanks go to my vision helpers who have contributed massively in birthing out God's vision and calling for my life. Thank you for your unfailing love, encouragement, counselling and prayers. May the good Lord bless you richly and reward your labour of love towards me in Jesus name. Amen.

I also want to thank iuniverse for their persistent handiwork in bringing this manuscript into its finished product. For without your steadfastness this book would not have come to its finished product.

Preface

Jane Eke is the author of the book titled Costly Discipleship. She is a teacher of the word and she is passionate about disciplining and building soldiers for God by teaching them how to exercise their authority in Christ, and also bringing people out of darkness into God's marvellous light. Jane studied business and management at a degree level and also completed a master in human resources management. She became interested in writing this book on how Christian's should exercise their authority over fear after discovering that the weapons that the devil uses to sabotage the destinies of God's children is the fear of the unknown. Hence, this has deprived and has rendered many Christian's unfit for purpose. The reason being that, fear has torment and it is also a killer of divine destiny. This is because it cripples and paralyzes individual's belief system by preventing them from stepping out of the known to the unknown; where the blessings of God await them. This book titled *'Exercising your Authority over Fear'* empowers Christian's on how to create their world through the power of the spoken word. This book teaches Christian's how to speak into being those things that are not as though they were. Furthermore, this book is also designed to help Christian's conquer their fears by enlightening humanity on the tactics they need to stand their ground against the wiles of the devil and how to exercise their authority in Christ. In addition, this book urges humanity to strive to break out of every stronghold that intends to obstruct their destiny. Moreover, this book outlines the consequences attached to fear such as missing the mark which in return separates you from God and also shows you how to prevent such from happening.

Introduction

Every great and successful man has to conquer his fears in order to unlock God's divine call and his destiny. Fear is a killer of destiny because it cripples and paralyzes your belief system. It is a tool that Satan uses to camouflage your God divine destiny. Fear indeed is an enemy of God and also of your destination. It thwarts God's children from freely possessing all that God has in store for them. Fear prevents God's children from stepping out of the known into the unknown. In this book exercising your authority over fear teaches believers how to conquer their fear by having faith in God. This book empowers you on how to create your world by speaking those things that are not as though they were. Furthermore, this book outline the consequences attached to fear such as missing the mark which in return separate you from God. This book also endows you with the knowledge you need to stand your ground against the wiles of the devil and how to exercise your authority in Christ. It highlights the importance of what it means to reign with Christ by renewing your mindset and taking hold of your destiny in Christ through the power of confession.

This book is designed to help you break out of every stronghold that wants to obstruct you from fulfilling destiny. This is because fear has torment and it has the capacity of depriving you of your true self-worth.

Our greatest enemy is not the external enemy but the enemy within (internal) i.e. your mind. This is because God will deal with your external enemy if you totally yield and surrender your lives and will to Him. But our greatest enemy is within because God has given us freedom of choice; and this fear has the ability to influence our choice i.e. our decisions; thereby, resulting to taking and making wrong decisions that will jeopardise your destiny and also cause you to compromise your stand for God. Fear cripples Christians' ability to step out of faith into God's predestined glory and future. Fear is also the tactics that the devil uses to stop God's children from launching out to the deep thereby rendering them unfruitful. This fear must be captured and dealt with; in other to fulfil your mandate and high calling in God; and this is what this book is designed to do for Christians and readers nationwide.

Jane Eke

Chapter 1 – What is Fear?

Fear is an act of the mind and if not probably dealt with has the capability of depriving Christians of their final destiny. Nations have missed their fate as a result of terror and their inability to replenish their mind. The Bible say: *"⁷For God did not give us a spirit of timidity (of cowardice, of craven and cringing and fawning fear), but*

> "Nations have missed their fate as a result of terror and their inability to replenish their mind".

[He has given us a spirit] of power and of love and of calm and well-balanced mind and discipline and self-control".[1] Christian's have to understand that we are on a battlefield and that the devil is constantly fighting us to destroy Christians from their divine purpose. One of the ways he does that is by putting fear in the hearts and minds of Christians. The excellent news is: *"God has not given his children the spirit of fear but of power and love".* The devil is aware that he cannot defeat God's children in battle; however, he still makes further attempts by putting sins in the hearts and minds of Christians. He does this by reminding Christians of their past sin, mistakes and misfortune. The Bible says: *"⁷I appeal to you therefore, brethren, and beg of you in view of [all] the mercies of God, to make a decisive dedication of your bodies [presenting all your members*

---

[1] 2 Timothy 1 vs. 7 AMP

and faculties] as a living sacrifice, holy (devoted, consecrated) and well pleasing to God, which is your reasonable (rational, intelligent) service and spiritual worship. ²Do not be conformed to this world (this age), [fashioned after and adapted to its external, superficial customs], but be transformed (changed) by the [entire] renewal of your mind [by its new ideals and its new attitude], so that you may prove [for yourselves] what is the good and acceptable and perfect will of God, even the thing which is good and acceptable and perfect [in His sight for you]. [2]

A Christian who fails to trust God by renewing his heart and understanding will potentially miss his divine plan. The mind is the front of every Christian; therefore, the devil uses this same reasoning to thwart their decision making; resulting in Christians executing wrong decisions. The reason why most Christians have missed it is because they believe the devil proposal as God's divine guidance. As the scriptures says: *"¹⁵study and be eager and do your utmost to present yourself to God approved (tested by trial), a workman who has no cause to be ashamed, correctly analyzing and accurately dividing [rightly handling and skilfully teaching] the Word of Truth"*[3]. In order for Christians to receive divine guidance and companionship from their Maker will require them to seek the Lord by tarrying in His presence, worshipping, praying and studying the word of God. The Bible says: *"My sheep hear my voice. I know them, and they follow me"*[4]. The disadvantage of not studying and meditating on God's word is that it deprives us of hearing God and dictating His voice. The word of God is an element and channel that

> *"In order for Christians to receive divine guidance and companionship from their Maker will require them to seek the Lord by tarrying in His presence, worshipping, praying and studying the word of God".*

---

[2] Romans 12 vs. 1-2 AMP
[3] 2 Timothy 2 vs. 15 AMP
[4] John 10 vs. 27 ISV

God uses to transfer knowledge and communicate the secret things, mysteries of His kingdom to His beloved children. A Christian that is too busy with the world's systems and its prosperity will potentially miss God when He decides to visit them.

Fear can be seen as a potential enemy because of various reasons. For example, people that are prayer warriors are likely not to accept temptation by the devil because they are extensively rooted in God and His word. Additionally, the devil is likely to experience disappointments on those who have revelational knowledge of God's word and also understand their authority in Christ. Furthermore, it is difficult for the devil to attract true Christians and worshippers of the Most High because they have an intimate relationship with God and they reverence Him. The devil is obliged to accept disappointments when tempting true Christians with lies, sin, unforgiveness, and backbiting because they know their authority in Christ and also know how to use their power over the devil. However, the devil may use terror to constrain such people. This is because fear cripples your belief system. It kills your faith and your ability to trust God and His word. The lesson here is that what we fail to deal with could emerge itself when we least expect it.

> "The lesson here is that what we fail to deal with could emerge itself when we least expect it".

Fear can also be defined as false evidence appearing real. In order to advance into your sacred destiny and promise land; Christians should be prepared to deal with their opposition called fear. An example of a man that fear took a grip on was Job in Job 3 vs. 25. The Bible says *"for the thing which I greatly fear comes upon me and that of which I am afraid*

> "God will not allow the devil to tempt us beyond what we can bear because He will always make a way of escape in the midst of storms".

befalls me"[5]. Job was a virtuous man who feared God and abstained from sin. Job was also the apple of God's eyes because he found favour with God. As a result, God also boasted about him to Satan. This made it difficult for Satan to tempt Him without God's authority. Additionally, Job was a righteous man because he daily woke up to offer sacrifices to God for himself and on behalf of his family. The food for thought from Job case; is that God will not allow the devil to tempt us beyond what we can bear because He will always make a way of escape in the midst of storms. Fear is a spirit, and that attitude must be conquered and subdued before Christians can enter into their rest. Job failed to subdue his flesh and spirit that is why fear gripped him. What do you fear the most? This is because the devil will haunt us with what we fear the most. If we fail to understand this, then ask Job.

The reason why what Job feared the most came upon him was because fear crippled his belief system, and also hindered his ability to believe and trust God. The Bible advices Christians: *"but the man who has doubts (misgivings, an uneasy conscience) about eating, and then eats [perhaps because of you], stands condemned [before God], because he is not true to his convictions and he does not act from faith. For whatever does not originate and proceed from faith is sin [whatever is done without a conviction of its approval by God is sinful]"*[6]. In other words, anything Christians fear the most opens the door for the devil to use it to haunt us. This is because when we fear something; it means that we doubt God's ability to be God in that area, and when we engage in such activity; we have stepped out of grace i.e. from God's covering and we have opened the door for the enemy to come in and afflict us.

Everyone has different phobias of different things; for some, it is the phobia of death, for others it is self-esteem and rejection, phobia of the

---

5 Job 3 vs. 25 AMP
6 Romans 14 vs. 23 AMP

unknown, and phobia of failure. Furthermore, some people might have a phobia of divorce, phobia of reoccurrence of their past, and phobia of flying. Whilst others have a phobia of success or of what people might say about them. The main issue is that we are all different, and people who are different also have different destinies as well as fears. To get into your pre-destination ordained by

> *"Fear is as a result of your past mistakes, failures, and worries. It is a strategic plan of the enemies to deter God's children by keeping them bound with fear and worries."*

God requires us to subdue and absorb that feeling of fear. However, failure to overcome your fear and deal with its origins will jeopardise your destiny and God's plan for your life. Fear is as a result of your past mistakes, failures, and worries. It is a strategic plan of the enemies to deter God's children by keeping us bound with fear and worries. This is because his plan is to prevent us, from pressing on and moving forward to achieve and embrace our desired plan. Fear must be conquered before Christians can perfectly move into their predetermined glory.

Two Kinds of Fear

Do you know that most people are suffering from an enemy called fear? Fear is an enemy because it causes mortality to reverence what they fear the most. There are two kinds of fear; the first being reverence for God. To fear God, means worshipping, respecting and reverencing Him; and the second one is the devil kind of fear. The Bible says: *"the reverent and worshipful fear of the Lord is the beginning*

> *"To fear God means to reverence Him and accept His Lordship over your life".*

(the chief and choice part) of wisdom, and the knowledge of the Holy one is insight and understanding"[7]. Another Bible passage says: *"the reverent fear and worship of the Lord is the beginning of wisdom and skill (the*

---

7 Proverbs 9 vs. 10 AMP

preceding and the first essential, the prerequisite and the alphabet); a good understanding, wisdom and meaning have all those who do the will of the Lord, their praise of Him endures forever"[8]. To fear God means to reverence Him and accept His Lordship over your life. For the Bible describes God's fear as wisdom, and Jesus Christ is wisdom personified. Fearing God gives us wisdom above your peers and contemporaries; as He did for King Solomon and Daniel who had an excellence spirit.

What does it mean to fear God

1 – *Loving God with all your heart, body and soul* – The Bible says: *"you shall love the Lord your God with all your heart, and with all your soul and with all your mind (intellect)"*[9]. The greatest commandment is to love God with all your heart and also love your neighbour as yourself. When we love someone we try to avoid hurting that person; the same thing applies in your relationship with God. For example, when a Christian says he/she loves God, they have to obey God's commandments and instructions as well as ensure that they separate themselves from anything that will keep God in second place, in their hearts and daily activities.

Loving God should not only be in words but also in deeds because many Christians only love God in words and not in reality. For instance, if we say that we love God, and we see a friend going through a challenging moment. The duty of Christians, is not only to pray for God's provision but also to be a blessing to our fellow brother if we have the resources because by so doing we have demonstrated your love for God. The Bible says that we shall know them by their fruits. In other words, the fruits that we must carry are illustrated in Galatians 5 vs. 22-23. The Bible says: *"but the fruits of the Holy Spirits (the works which His*

---

[8] Psalms 111 vs. 10 AMP
[9] Matthew 22 vs. 37-38 AMP

presence within accomplishes) is love, joy (gladness), peace, patience (an even temper, forbearance), kindness, goodness (benevolence), faithfulness, gentleness (meekness, humility), self-control (self –restraint, continence)"[10]. In other words, these above fruits must become a norm in the life of a Christian i.e. become part of your daily life, conduct, words and deeds towards others. Also, in order to love others we must love God first because He gives us the ability to love others as we love ourselves.

2- **Acknowledges His Lordship in your life** – Fear of God causes humanity to reverence God and accept His Lordship over their lives. This is because God knew us and predestined us before the foundation of the world. By acknowledging God's Lordship, we are surrendering our all to Him. In other words, Christian's are laying down their preference for His. Jesus paid the price to save

> *"Acknowledging God in everything we do guarantees divine supervision and protection".*

humanity back to Himself by shedding His blood on the cross of Calvary. God bought us with a price, hence; Christian's should always acknowledge Him in everything they do such as in their daily activities, decision making and daily plans. Failing to include God in your daily activities may result in misery because all things consist in Him and nothing is made without Him. Christian's daily activities must be embedded on the solid Rock because the Lord Jesus Christ never fails. This is because when the storms come to ruin your future aspirations and plans, it will not fail because He is the Rock that never fails. Acknowledging God in everything we do guarantees divine supervision and protection.

Failing to incorporate God in your daily activities and decision making, can be likened to a man writing a letter and forgetting to include God before posting his letter. Obviously, that letter may or may not reach

---

10 Galatians 5 vs. 22-23 AMP

its destination because there is a probability that the stamp will not be sufficient for the journey. This means that for a man to get to their destination in life; he cannot afford to eliminate God in his daily activities and decisions. The choice we make on a daily basis affects Christians tomorrow (destiny) and the people connected to them by divine providence. Therefore, Christians should be extremely careful in everything they do because it has the habit of making them or perhaps breaking them. For that reason, a Christian cannot afford not to accept God's Lordship over their lives. If not, they are heading towards death and destruction.

As a Christian, it is either we fear God or Satan (the devil). The truth of the matter is that whomever we fear we automatically reverence. For example, a Christian that fears that he/she will fail his/her exams might even end up failing his/her exams because that person has crippled and starved both their faith and their belief system. Hence, given reverence to the devil. The Bible says: "*for as he thinks in his heart, so is he*"[11]. The devil is just waiting for Christians to think it, so that he can help them accomplish it. Another example is someone who fears to get married because they are afraid of divorce; that alone, has given the devil a foothold to oppress them. Christians would need to deal with its origin and its cause in order to be liberated. The truth is that fear is an enemy to your greater height. The devil introduces fear into the hearts and minds of Christians in order to restrain them from obtaining their promise and enter into their rest. As the

> *"The devil introduces fear into the hearts and minds of Christians in order to restrain them from obtaining their promise and enter into their rest."*

scripture stated "*for he who has once entered [God's] rest also has ceased from [the weariness and pain] of human labours, just as God rested from*

---

[11] Proverbs 23 vs. 7 AMP

those labours [f]peculiarly His own. [11]Let us therefore be zealous, and exert ourselves and strive diligently to enter that rest [of God, to know and experience it for ourselves], that no one may fall or perish by the same kind of unbelief and disobedience [into which those in the wilderness fell]".[12]

Another example is a Christian who had a horrible past relationship and fears that entering into a new one could bring back their past reoccurrence. The person involved has failed to learn from their past mistakes as well as has also refused to open the door of their hearts for Master Jesus to nurse, nurture, support and equip them. Hence, they go about in their daily activities assuming that they would be healed from their past, but in reality, they struggle with emotional instability. Christian's in such manner will find it difficult to grow in the things of the kingdom because they have given the devil a foothold in their lives. Furthermore, Christian's must deal with their stronghold in order to obtain their promises. Fear is an enemy, and the enemy must be dealt with if they want to enjoy what God has in store for them.

Ignorance is a disease and some people might be naive to the fact that they are harbouring fear in them. The Bible says: examine and test and evaluate your own selves to see whether you are holding to your faith and showing the proper fruits of it. Test and prove yourselves [[a]not Christ]. Do you not yourselves realize and know [thoroughly by an ever-increasing experience] that Jesus Christ is in you--unless you are [counterfeits] disapproved on trial and rejected"[13]? When Christians engages in daily self-examination they have privileges of God exposing areas of their lives that needs correction. This prevents the devil from gaining a foothold in their life. If a Christian, assumes that all is well when it is not; he is likely to be caught unaware. The Bible says: "therefore, let anyone who thinks he stands [who feels sure that he has a

---

12 Hebrews 4 vs. 10-11 AMP
13 2 Corinthians 13 vs. 5 AMP

steadfast mind and is standing firm], take heed lest he fall [into sin]"[14]. The devil is your enemy, and his role in Christian's life is to "steal and kill and destroy"[15]. The devil does not want your satisfaction but wants to kill your vision and destiny in God. It is

> *"To walk in divine purpose Christians need to encounter Jesus Christ and the Holy Ghost".*

necessary to secure every entry which may permit the devil logging into your life. This can be done by praying and asking God to *"reveal to you any door that you have open to the devil out of ignorance"*. God in His infinite mercy because of His faithfulness will answer your prayers, but we need to be sensitive to His leading. The devil has blinded the eyes of many Christian's; thus, they are insensitive to the leading of God. As

> *"The devil does not want your satisfaction but wants to kill your vision and destiny in God".*

the scripture says: *"for the god of this world has blinded the unbelievers' minds [that they should not discern the truth], preventing them from seeing the illuminating light of the Gospel of the glory of Christ (the Messiah), who is the Image and Likeness of God"[16].* Christians should also be wise and cautious because your adversary the devil roams about like a roaring lion seeking whom he may devour.

3 - *Realigning yourself to His Perfect will* – Fearing God compiles Christians to strive to obey God by walking in their divine will of God for their lives. Also, fearing God causes Christian's to love and reverence Him by refusing to compromise their standards. Walking in the divine

> *"Fearing God causes Christian's to love and reverence Him by refusing to compromise their standards".*

will of God is one of the ways of pleasing God. For example, Peter was

[14] 1 Corinthians 10 vs. 12 AMP
[15] John 10 vs. 10a AMP
[16] 2 Corinthians 4 vs. 4 AMP

a fisherman, but when he encountered God; God reinstated his destiny as a fisher of men. Peter assumed that his only reasons for being were to become a fisherman. It took divine rearrangement and encounter from God to activate his divine providence as a fisher of men. Peter was only able to walk in the divine purpose after his divine encounter with Jesus Christ and the Holy Ghost. Fearing God causes humanity to meet with divinity; thereby, discovering their true identity in Christ and their divine assignment. The only way Christian's can realize their true identity in Christ is by encountering God for themselves. Certainly, there may be occasions where men and women of God may be able to tell us what your assignment is in the Lord. However, it is the responsibility of every Christian to seek the face of God because the moment we start depending on men; it exposes us to witchcraft manipulation.

It is essential for God's ordained servants to confirm God's words in your life, but it is the role of every Christian to get closer to God and know Him for themselves. This is because the devil is now in power and could be used to prognosticate wrongly into the lives of Christian's; hence, resulting in Christian's aborting their divine destiny. In matters regarding your divine assignment; we need to encounter God for ourselves and allow God to use His servant to confirm it, if He so

> *"The only way Christian's can realize their true identity in Christ is by encountering God for themselves because the moment you start depending on men; it exposes us to witchcraft manipulations.".*

pleases. Additionally, when Christians fear God they strive to ensure that they spend quality time in His presence. One of the benefits of spending quality time in God's presence is that His personality rubs off on us. There is a proverb that says *"show me your friend, and I will tell you who you are"*. When Christian's call Jesus their friend, and they derive happiness in fellowshipping with Him; sooner or later we think, see, speak and do things the way He does. Another thing to be aware of is: *"bad companies corrupt good morals"*. Peter encounter with God not only realigned him to God's will for his life but also activated it.

Many Christians are ignorant and are without vision. The Bible says: *"my people are destroyed for lack of knowledge"*[17]. It will amaze us to know that many Christians do not know the will of God for their lives; thus, they are toss through and fro, left and right. Such individuals can be likened as victims that jump to any bus going to any destination.

Christians are unstable in the doctrines of Christ because they are toss by every wind of doctrine. This is because their reasoning is vague as a result of lack of knowledge in the things of God. The scripture says *"there is a way which seemeth right unto a man, but the end thereof are the ways of death"*[18]. Christians in such classification would require a divine encounter from God, because He alone can realign us back to His will. Many have also missed it because of disobedience to God; the Bible says *"to obey is better than sacrifice"*[19].

Missing the mark can never be underestimated especially when running the race for God but the good news is that God does not look at your past mistakes, and misery when we restitute. God forgives and shows mercy on His children when they retrace their steps back to Him. For instance, Apostle Paul a tax collector was hostile towards Christian's by sending

> *"The lesson for those underestimating themselves and writing themselves off is that it's not over until God say so".*

some to their early grave. However, when he encountered Master Jesus, his life changed and his purposed where redefined and activated. Despite Paul's past atrocities; God still used him in his generation. The lesson

---

17 Hosea 4:6 AMP
18 Proverbs 14:12 KJV
19 1 Samuel 15:22 AMP

for those underestimating themselves and writing themselves off is that it is not over until God says so.

God specialises in using the foolish things to confound the wise; by using your past atrocities' as a message to the world. He does that to show off His glory as well as prove to the world that He specialises in the affairs of men. King David is another Bible character who killed and committed so much bloodshed but God still regarded him as *"a man after His heart"*[20]. This illustrates the fact that God's ways are past finding out and He does as it pleases. Men certainly look at the outward appearance, but God looks at the heart. In other words, men will always judge us based on what they can see, but God looks at the heart. It

> *"God doesn't always call the qualified but the unqualified to qualify".*

is necessary to shun from listening to men's judgement, but instead we should ensure that we have a right standing with God. It is necessary to note that one with God is stronger than a majority against us. For example, if David had written himself off maybe we would not have heard of him today. God does not always call the qualified, but the unqualified to qualify. Hence, our past mistakes and background are irrelevant to where God is taking us. God uses our past mistakes as a stepping stone to attaining greater heights in Him. Stop disqualifying yourself, but rather seek His face and not His gifts so that He can unravel your true identity in Him as well as activate it.

4- Seeking Him and spending quality time – God created us in the first place because he delights in your fellowship. Spending quality time seeking His face is what He desires from us. Fellowshipping with God gives us the grace to walk in the divine plan and it also nurtures, fortifies and equips us for His divine assignment. Christian's

---

[20] Acts 13:22 AMP

opens the door of their lives and heart to the devil when the desert from spending quality time in His presence. There is a divine protection and security that comes in dwelling in the secret place of the Most High. The Bible says: "he that dwelleth in the secret place of the most high shall abide under the shadow of the Almighty"[21]. God is also your hiding place; He protects us from anxiety and gives us a song of deliverance. He is also equally ready to hide us from the intrigues of men. His hiding place will also keep us safe from accusing tongues. Even though, God is your Refuge and Shield; we still need to have faith in His word. This can only be done by fellowshipping in His presence and allowing Him to disclose His word to us. Another benefit that comes with spending quality time in God's presence is that He also unveils the mysteries of His kingdom to His children. He does that by revealing impeding dangers and His forthcoming blessings when we linger in His presence. The imminent dangers are not to frighten us. What it means is that it is your responsibility to denounce, dismiss and eradicate the imminent dangers through fasting and prayers as well as praying into speedily manifestation His forthcoming blessing.

5 – *Fear of the Lord is the beginning of wisdom* – Wisdom is the application of knowledge. God is the epitome of wisdom and for us to work in divine wisdom requires us to know God and respect Him. There are two types of wisdom; the first is the wisdom of God, and following is the philosophy

> *"God is the Lord and He is mighty in power; because His understanding has no limit. God is so great that He is able to turn fortified cities into piles of stones".*

of the world. The wisdom of the world has limits, but the wisdom of God is infinite. There is no searching of His understanding and the

---

21 Psalms 91:1 KJV

depths of the wealth of wisdom and knowledge of God! How unsearchable are His judgements because His paths is beyond tracing out. For example, before the mountains were formed i.e. even when we were born into the world, or the world itself, God was God; from everlasting to everlasting His God. God is vast and worthy to be praise because no one can comprehend His greatness (wisdom). Great is the Lord, and He is mighty in power; because His wisdom has no limit. God is so powerful that He turned fortified cities into piles of stones. He is the only one that can establish justice on earth because He uses the foolish things to confound the wise. God does as it pleases Him; He is unquestionable. God was designated from heaven, from the beginning, before the world began. The greatest wisdom a man should have is the wisdom of God because it derives from studying His words in His presence and fellowshipping with Him. The world assumes that worldly knowledge such as education is the ladder to

> *"Getting wisdom is the wisest thing you can do; and whatever else you do, develop sound judgement".*

attaining wisdom but that is the world's knowledge. Although, the wisdom of God is superior to the wisdom of men (world); thus, God many at times uses the wisdom of men and renders it foolishness; just to let them know that there is no searching of His wisdom and His wisdom has no limit; it's extremely enormous. Getting wisdom is the wisest thing to do and whatever else we do, develop sound judgement. Christians should get the truth and sell it not, get wisdom, discipline and understanding. Additionally, Christians have to walk in wisdom and understanding and forsake not or swerve not His precepts.

The Bible says that we should not deceive ourselves because if we want to become wise in the world we must be willing to become a fool for Christ, so that we may be wise. This is because the wisdom of the world is foolishness with God. *"For it is written, He takes the wise in their own craftiness"*[22]. The Lord certainly knows that the thoughts of the wise are futile. So we should strive not to glory in people because all things are ours in Christ Jesus.

---

[22] 1 Corinthians 3:19 KJV

Chapter 2 – What is Faith?

The greatest weapon of warfare used to overcome fear and the kingdom of darkness is faith, and faith is the absence of fear. As the scriptures say: *"faith is the confidence that what we hope for will actually happen; it gives us assurance about things we cannot see"*[23]. Faith is a necessary tool used to unlock any God given blessings. Faith is the middle man between your promise and your manifestation i.e. *"and it is impossible to please God without faith. Anyone who wants to come to him must believe that God exists and that he rewards those who sincerely seek him."*[24]. Faith helps us to communicate with our Maker because it enables us to believe His word and wait patiently on Him.

> *"Faith is a necessary tool used to unlock any God given blessings. Faith is the middle man between your promise and your manifestation".*

This feature called faith fortifies your relationship with God. For instance, we need faith to activate our destiny and trust God's word against all odd even if all hell is breaking loose. Activating our faith in God will give us victory over any circumstances and the sky will be our stepping stone. The Bible says: *"for in this hope we were save. But hope that is seen is not hope at all. Who hopes for what he already*

---

23 Hebrews 11:1 NLT
24 Hebrews 11:6 NLT

has?[25]We are to live by faith and not by sight. Christian's should not fix their eyes on what is seen but on what is unseen because what is seen is temporary and what is not seen is eternal. We should also seek to hold on to our faith in God which is our belief and anchor. This is because we are not of those who shrink back and are destroyed, but of those who believe and are saved.

Faith is one of the keys to the kingdom of God. This is because we need faith to believe God's word until it comes to fruition. Without faith, it is difficult to please God. It was by faith that Noah was cautioned by God of the things that he had not yet seen, and he was frightened to prepare an ark to save his entire family. It was also by Faith that Abraham was called out from his own kin into a place where he would receive his godly heritage. Abraham obeyed God even when he could not trace God. Many Christian's have withered away from faith because they gave in to the wiles of the devil when they could not trace God. It was by faith that Abraham sojourned into a land of promise as in a strange country. We were told that Abraham did not settle for less, but he looked for a city which has foundations, and who's Builder and Maker was God. It was also through faith that Sarah received strength to conceive when she had passed her menopause stage. Indeed, without faith how can we please God or even receive from Him. Brethren, it was also by this same faith that women received their dead raised back to life.

> "Many Christian's have withered away from faith because they gave in to the wiles of devil when they could not trace God"

Others, where tortured but refused to accept deliverance but instead chose to gain a better resurrection in Christ. Many Christians will not get anything from God because as the scripture says: *"for let not the*

---

25 Romans 8:24 NIV

man thinks that he will receive anything of the Lord[26]. *"Their loyalty is divided between God and the world, and they are unstable in everything they do"*[27]. God expects His children to walk in faith even when the storms of life seem to dominate them. This is because God is willing to still all the storms of life, but we must first believe in Him by activating our faith.

God expects us to trust Him because when we trust Him; He will always show up for us. He promised not to leave us or forsake us. Christians have to be strong and courageous. Be not afraid or terrified because of evildoers. This is because God is with us and has promised not to leave us or forsake us. Additionally, the Lord will go before us and will also be with us. He will never leave us nor forsake us; so do not be afraid or discourage. God is not unjust to abandon us or even ignore the covenant He had with your forefathers, which He confirms to them by oath. This indeed is what makes Him a king and a merciful God. Furthermore, the earlier we know that no one will be able to stand against us all the days of our life the better it is for us. God has given His promise to us that as He was with Moses so shall He be with us. He promised not to leave us nor forsake us. Even though, we may be persecuted, but can never be abandoned; struck down but never destroyed because God is with us.

Traits for Selfish Gains

It is necessary to note that Christians should not turn their hearts to selfish gains but rather to know God's status. Many Christians believe in God and have faith in God for worldly things and self ambitions. As the scripture says: "you have to seek the kingdom of God above all else, and live righteously, and He will give you everything you need"[28].

---

26 James 1:7 TBS
27 James 1:8 NLT
28 Matthew 6:33 NLT

Christian's should not be obsessed in accumulating mundane things. In other words, they should not indulge themselves into getting rich; but have the wisdom to show restraint. Christians should avoid storing up treasures for themselves here on earth; where mort and rust destroy

> *"Christians should not be obsessed in accumulating mundane things but have the wisdom to show restraint".*

and where thieves break in and steal. In other words, Christians should strive to put to death things belonging to human nature such as sexual immorality, impurities, lusts, evil desires and greed which is idolatry. They should not be given to drunkenness, but be gentle and not aggressive, and they should neither be quarrelsome or lovers of money.

Christians should be content with what they have. This is because *"godliness with contentment is great gain"*[29]. The psalmist says: *"I was young, and now I am old, yet I have never seen the righteous forsaken or their children begging bread"*[30]. How can we be in deficit when God is the God of abundance; who promises to provide all your needs according to His riches in glory? It is the possibility of being in need that pushes Christians to be obsessed with worldly things in the expense of their soul. As a result, many Christians believe in God and have faith

> *"Christian's believe God and have faith in God for the wrong things; just to satisfy their earthly and selfish desires".*

in God for the wrong things; just to satisfy their sensual and selfish desires. Thus, God many a times will not answer the request of His children especially those that are indulging in selfish and materialistic ambitions. God promises to lead the blind in the ways they have not known; along unfamiliar paths, he will lead them. He also promises to turn their darkness into light and make their rough places smooth. The

---

[29] 1 Timothy 6:6 NIV
[30] Psalms 37:25 NIV

question is: why are we believing God and having faith in God for the wrong things?

God's Faithfulness

One thing Christians should know is that wealth and prosperity are in God's house, and His righteousness endures forever. God also has wealth and honour in His hands and enduring wealth and prosperity. The Lord will never let His own children go hungry. These is because the blameless will always receive substantial inheritance; indeed if we believe Him and have faith in Him the abundance of the sea shall be converted unto us; the forces of the gentiles shall come unto us. Christians should covet and thirst for more of God; this is because those that seek Him early will find Him.

Faith Definition

1 -*Faith assures us of things we want and convinces us of the reality of things we cannot see* - In other words, when we make our request known; we hereby believe in God for the fulfilment regardless of our current situation or predicaments. As the scriptures says: *"and this is the confidence that we have in him that, if we ask anything according to his will, He hearth us"*[31]. Faith enables us to see ourselves in possession of what we have asked from God even before we actually see the physical manifestation of our request. In order to receive anything from God; we have to ask according to His will and purpose for your lives. Our prayers will not be approved by God if it does not align to God divine will. There are three answers that God gives His

> *"Faith assures us of the promises of God for our lives and also helps us to continue to depend on Him until we see Him materialise His promises".*

---

[31] 1 John 5:14 TSB

children i.e. Yes, No or Wait. When God says 'Yes', – it means that what we have asked Him is in line with His divine will, but we have to wait for His timing. The answer 'No' – means that our request are outside His divine will for us thus, He disapproves our request. Finally, the answer 'Wait' – means that our requests are in line with His divine plan for your lives; but we have to undergo some spiritual and psychological training in order to manage that which He has in store for us. As the scriptures says *"but as it is written, eye hath not seen, nor ear heard, neither have entered into the heart of man, the things which God hath prepared for them that love him"[32]. "God's thoughts are nothing like your thoughts," says the Lord. "And my ways are far beyond anything you could imagine"[33].* God's plans for our life stand forever because no one can prevent it or even modify it. This is because as He speaks it is settled. Faith assures us of the promises of God for our lives and also helps us to continue to depend on Him until we see Him materialise His promises.

2 – *Faith is the spiritual eyes we need to obtain your promise* – Faith is the eyes that see the promise of God come into manifestation in the realm of the spirit, before it actually materialises in the physical. Faith in God energies our spirit to be in tune with God's spirit, and thereby causes us to see things from God's perspective. Christians need to activate their faith in God before they can obtain their inheritance in Christ and also receive all that God has in store for them. For example, in the Bible Jesus cursed the fig tree because he was a man of faith.

> *"Faith in God energies our spirit to be in tune with God's spirit, and thereby causes us to see things from God's perspective".*

The scripture says: *"In the morning, when they were passing along, they noticed that the fig tree was withered [completely] away to its roots. And Peter remembered and said to Him, Master, look! The fig tree which you*

---

[32] 1 Corinthians 2: 9 KJV
[33] Isaiah 55:8 NLT

doomed has withered away! And Jesus, replying, said to them, Have faith in God [constantly]. Truly I tell you, whoever says to this mountain, be lifted up and thrown into the sea! And does not doubt at all in his heart but believes that what he says will take place, it will be done for him. For this reason I am telling you, whatever you ask for in prayer, believe (trust and be confident) that it is granted to you, and you will [get it]³⁴.

God promises that whatever we ask the Father in His name He will do it. This means that for us to move mountains and trust God to bring His promise concerning our life to prominence requires us to activate our faith. Without faith, it is difficult to please God. This is because God needs His children to take Him to His words. When God's children doubt God, what they are telling God is that He is not a man of His words and He is unfit to perform His words. God hates this because it damages His integrity. Thus, God says that we cannot have an established relationship with Him if we do not trust in Him. The same thing goes in your relationships with men and men's relationships with women; we cannot have a lasting relationship with them if we do not learn to trust each other and have faith in each other. Faith helps us to stay focused on God despite all odds. This is what it means to keep an eye in the spirit, i.e. spiritual eyesight. This spiritual eyesight stirs up our faith in God in such a way that we refuse to give up on our current predicaments. Christians should be encouraged to keep on pushing through the dirt because they believe God and His words. Brethren, our faith needs to be activated in order for us to do greater exploits for God as well as, fulfil destiny in God. This is because it is one thing to receive the word of promise and it is another thing to have faith in the word thereby seeing the word become a reality.

The same thing applies to people who have great assignments from God. When the going gets tough especially during difficult

---

34 Mark 11 vs. 20-24 AMP

oppositions, as a result of our assignment; we need to rely solely on God and have faith in Him. The Bible admonishes us *"through faith we understand that the worlds were framed by the word of God, so that things which are seen are not made of things which do appear"*[35]. This means that faith is indeed an essential tool for kingdom business. God used faith to frame the world around Him. How much more we that are living in this world? A corresponding Bible verse says:*"so we don't look at the troubles we can see now; rather, we fix our gaze on things that cannot be seen. For the things we see now will soon be gone, but the things we cannot see will last forever"*[36]. This means that we should focus on God and

> "When the going gets tough especially during oppositions as a result of our assignment; you need to rely solely on God and have faith in Him. Christian's should focus on God and not our problems; one of the ways to focus on God is by exercising our faith in God and over our predicaments".

not on our problems; one of the ways to focus on God is by exercising our faith in God and over your predicaments. The Bible says that we were saved in this hope. But hope seen is not hope at all. Who hope's for what he already has?

Christians should remember that we are saved by faith and faith alone, and we live by faith and not by sight. For example, because of Enoch's relationship with God; he did not experience death but was taken by God. By faith, Abel offered a better sacrifice than Cain and he was counted as righteous. Additionally, by faith Noah built an ark for God. Christians need faith to walk with God and also fulfil their assignments. Noah could only walk in his divine assignment by activating his faith in God. This shows that a man that fails to activate his/her faith in God is bound to be unfilled in life because the scriptures says a double minded man is unstable and cannot receive anything from God. In addition

---

35 Hebrews 11:3 ASV
36 2 Corinthians 4:18 NLT

to this, we ask and do not receive because we ask amiss, that we may consume it upon your own lust.

3 – *We need faith to enter into another dimension* – One of the benefits of entering into another dimension is that we cease to perceive things carnally. The Bible says: *"for to be carnally minded is death; but to be spiritually minded is life and peace. Because the carnal mind is enmity against God; for it is not subject to the law of God, neither indeed can be. So then they that are in the flesh cannot please God[37].* When a Christian is obsessed by carnal mentality, they are likely to execute wrong decisions. Such people are also likely to listen to people that are willing to starve and destroy their faith rather than strengthen it.

> "God promised that all those who rage against you will surely be put to shame and disgraced, and those that opposed you will have no choice than to perish".

Therefore, in order to tap into another dimension in God requires a high level of confidence and obedience. These two go together because without faith, it is difficult to please God. Secondly, we need faith to obey God even when we cannot trace Him. Faith is required in order to obtain His magnificent promises. The Bible also says: *"they that are in the flesh cannot please God"[38].* Christian's cannot please God when they are operating from the flesh. They need to connect to the spirit in order to download the mysteries of God's kingdom as well as all that He has in store for them. When praying; one of the benefits of faith is that it causes us to see things from a spiritual perspective. Faith also

> "When a Christian is consumed by carnal mentality they are likely to execute wrong decisions. Such people are also likely to listen to people that are willing to starve and destroy their faith rather than strengthen it."

---

37 Romans 8:6-8 TBS
38 Romans 8:8 KJV

enables us to tap into the spiritual realm of God; in order to see all that God has in store for us before we actually possess it.

4 – *Faith enables us to govern your world* – Faith certainly helps us govern our world because Christians needs to prevail over their spiritual world in order to be victorious in the earthly realm. This is because the invisible (i.e. spiritual realm) control the physical realm (i.e. the mortal realm). Faith that conquers is a faith that is solidly engulfed in the Lord Jesus Christ. It is a faith that refuses to give up against all odds, trials and persecution. Faith that conquers is a faith that is rooted and grounded in God and His word. This is the reason why the Bible says to let the word of God dwell in us richly because the word of God helps to superimpose the will of God in our life, family and loved ones. When we come into agreements with God regarding any issue the devil is in trouble even though he will try to fight against it. Surely he will never prevail against it. The scripture says: *"If any nation comes to fight you, it is not because I sent them. Whoever attacks you will go down in defeat"*[39]. Indeed your enemies will conspire against you and watch your steps in order to take your life. God promises that all those who rage against us will certainly be put to shame and disgraced, and those that opposed us will have no choice than to perish. The eyes of the spirit help us to take hold of what belongs to us which the devil has stolen. It also gives us the power to decree divine judgement against the camp of our enemies and God will approve it. This is because He said if we ask anything in His name He will do it.

5 – *Faith activates your blessing and favour from God* – Faith is the credential required to possess our possession. It is the fuel we need to act on God's word. This faith is well-known as having confident and trust in God, knowing that He can do just what He says He will do. God is a God of more than enough. Christians that are operating in faith has no

[39] Isaiah 54:15 NLT

limits or boundaries of what they can receive from God. This is because they know how to trust, act and obey God's word by confessing His promises back to Him. The Lord cannot withhold any pleasant thing from them. God's expectation for us is not only to understand the promise

> *"Faith is the credential required to possess our possession. It is the fuel we need to act on God's word".*

but also to act on it by confessing it. The scripture says that we should speak those things that be not as though they were. God expects us to create our world with the promise He has given us through His word.

It is not enough to have received the word and then fold our arms expecting God to bring it to pass. This is because we need to fight for what is ours; the fact that God has given us the word does not mean that the devil will not fight against the word. As the scripture says we will have to contend with the prince of the kingdom of Persia; some people will have to contend with principalities, against powers, against rulers of darkness of this world, against spiritual wickedness in high places. God created and framed this world by the spoken word of God; so that things which are seen were not made of things which do appear. Likewise, God expects us to use our authority in Christ by declaring the word of God in our current predicaments. God also wants us to declare what we see in the realm of the spirit and not what we see in the earthly realm. God expects us to have a positive confession regardless of our predicaments. God's word is settled forever in heaven, and His words are yes and amen. In other words, once He spoke it, it is settled. All He is just waiting for is the appointed time to bring the promise to fruition.

6 – *Faith originates from the word of God* – Faith is connected to the word of God because the promises of God are in His word. In other words, whatever we want from God be it promotion, good health, sound mind, academic excellence, divine protection and provision,

breakthrough, and upliftment are all in the word of God. Christians responsibility is to go back to the word of God and search the scriptures that link to the areas they are trusting in God. Then declare it into materialisation and it will come to pass if they doubt not. For instance, if we trust God to give us wisdom; all we need do is ask the God who gave it to King Solomon because if He gave it to King Solomon, He can also give it to us. Or maybe we trust the Lord for good health; He wishes us good health so that we might prosper. Furthermore, if it is excellence spirit we trust God to provide; we could ask the God of Daniel. Maybe it is promotion that we trust God to give us: my Bible tells me that promotion comes only from God because He can pick a beggar from a dunghill and place him before

> *"Faith is the modem that we use to transmit and download coded information from the realm of the spirit. It enables us to commune with God".*

the prince and kings. Additionally, it could be that we are trusting God for business expansion and enlargement. My Bible tells me that God gives us the ability to get wealth. God is willing to give us success, as well as fight all our battles. God is also ready to restore our soul; as well as preserve our going and coming. God is indeed the God of abundance. The word of God is our manual for life and in it lies all the promises of God. All we need do is ask God, and you will receive, that our joy may be full. God is indeed the stiller all storms of life; so why not trust Him with your life.

Finally, faith is the modem that we use to transmit and download coded information from the realm of the spirit. Faith enables us to commune with God. The Bible says that without faith, it is impossible to please Him. Faith enables us to understand the things that God has freely given to us as well as helps us in our daily walk with Him. Faith is one of the keys of the kingdom of God because everything originates from faith in God. Now the question is do you have faith in God? Do you believe Him to be God over your life? Do you trust Him to bring to pass all that He has promised you? If not, we should take a moment and restitute our ways by asking Him to forgive us and have mercy on us so that we can be reinstated back to our original inheritance in Christ right before the foundation of the world.

Chapter 3 – The Consequences of Fear

The absence of faith is fear and it stops us from receiving our inheritance in Christ Jesus. Fear has consequences because for some, it might prevent them from obtaining their promise and even enter their rest. The Bible says that fear has torment. God has not given us a spirit that enslaves us to fear; we have received the spirit of sonship, whereby we cry Abba Father. Moreover, the scriptures says: *"for God did not give us a spirit of timidity (of cowardice, of craven and cringing and fawning fear), but [He has given us a spirit] of power and of love and of calm and well-balanced mind and discipline and self-control"* [40]. Brethren, if God is your light and your salvation, why should we fear? If God is your refuge and stronghold why should we also be afraid of our enemies? The wicked shall come to kill our flesh, but they would stumble and fall because the Lord is our stay and we will not fear what people will do to us.

> *"Brethren, if God is your light and your salvation, why should we fear? If God is our refuge and stronghold why should we also be afraid of our enemies?"*

---

[40] 2 Timothy 1:7 AMP

God assures us not to be afraid because He will be with us at all times. He said that we should not be dismayed with the fear that surrounds us because He is there to support us and fight for us. This is because all those that conspire against us will be ashamed and disgraced, and all those that fight with us shall perish and come to nothing because God is our Redeemer, the Holy One of Israel will hold our right hand to help us in times of trouble. God also

> *"God promises to be our God when we pass through the storms of life. He promises that the storms of life will not overpower us because He is there with us and He will also be our fireproof".*

promises to be our God when we pass through the storms of life. He promised that the storms of life will not overpower us; He said that even though we find ourselves in the fiery furnace like Shadrach, Meshach and Abednego that not only will He be there with us; but He will also be our fireproof.

God is our Saviour and He is always ready to deliver us from the snare of the fowler. God even assures us that a thousand may fall both on our left and right side, but they will not come near us. We will only observe them with our own eyes and see the rewards of the wicked. If only we could stand firm, be strong and courageous and be not afraid of the terror of the enemies because God has promised that He will never leave us nor forsake us. Remember the account of Moses and the children of Israel when Moses told the children of Israel: *"fear not; stand still (firm, confident, undismayed) and see the salvation of the Lord which He will work for you today. For the Egyptians you have seen today you shall never see again. The Lord will fight for you and you shall hold your peace and remain at rest"*[41]. From this account, God did not only give them victory but also drowned their enemies in the red seas. God says we should not let our hearts be agitated, but we should learn to believe and rely on Him

---

[41] Exodus 14:13-14 AMP

because He has promised not to leave us comfortless. How much more victory will He give to those who He has bought with a price?

The Consequences of Fear

The dilemma facing God's children is that they give the devil hearing ears; hence, the devil uses several strategies to manipulate them. An example is when God's children indulge in daily sin or maybe miss the mark. The Bible says: *"whatsoever is not of faith is sin"*[42]. It will amaze us to know that many Christians claim to believe in God and claim His promises for their lives, but in reality, they are walking in despair. The devil comes into the life of Christians to steal the word of God that is sown in their hearts. This is done

> *"The dilemma facing God's children is that they give the devil hearing ears; hence, the devil uses several strategies to manipulate them".*

by giving the devil a hearing ears, thus, he starves them with doubt rather than encourage their faith. Another set of people, are the people who have received the word of God with gladness in their hearts, but when the persecution arises on account of the word it withers away because the word sown in their hearts has no root in them i.e. the word has not become part of their subconsciousness. Hence, they lose it when the devil attacks the word and their faith.

Furthermore, some people lose the word that God has given to them because they are after the cares of the world. Christian's main concern is how they can obtain the world's recognition and attractiveness in the expense of their soul. What will it profit a man to gain the world and lose his soul in the kingdom of God? This is all part of the devil's plans because he knows that we have become a terror to his kingdom; hence, he put all kinds of strategies in place so as to get God's children to drift

---

42 Romans 14:23 KJV

away from Him and settle for counterfeit instead of God's perfect will. This people are the people that the word was sown among thorns. Such people have allowed the cares of the world, the deceits of richness, and the lust of other things to choke the word that God has given them; hence, rendering God's word in such an individual as unfruitful. But Christians who hear the word and keep it, thereby bringing forth fruits, some thirtyfold, some sixty and some hundred are those in which the word was sown in good ground.

Whether you like it or not the devil will fight you. The Bible warns us *"to be alert watch out for your great enemy, the devil. He prowls around like a roaring lion, looking for someone to devour"*[43]. Christian's should be vigilant of their deadly enemy called Satan, so that he might not outsmart them because they are unaware of his schemes. Additionally, Christian's should therefore, prepare their hearts and minds for action; they have to be self-controlled and set their hope on the grace that is given to them by God. It was fear that got Zacharias to question God thereby doubting God Almightiness. This rendered him dumb until the day the promise came to prominence. The Bible says that we should keep watch because we do not know the day that the Lord will come. *"The Lord is not slack concerning His promise as men count slackness; but is longsuffering to usward, not willing that any should perish, but that all should come to repentance. But the day of the Lord will come as a thief in the night"*[44].

Also, doubt and cynicism is another strategy which devil uses to deceive God's children. The Bible says that even Jesus could not perform miracles in his home town, because of unbelief as the scripture says that a prophet is without honour in his family and home town. It is fear that causes God's children to walk in doubt to God's word and His promises concerning their lives. The word of God says that when

---

43 1 Peter 5:8 NLT
44 2 Peter 3:9-10 TBS

we ask God for something, we should have faith in God alone. The moment we start wavering and doubting; we are likened to a person that has divided loyalty and such a person are unsettled, as a wave of the sea that is blown and tossed by the wind. Such a person will not be able to receive anything from the Lord, because his loyalties are divided between God and the world, and he is also unstable in everything he does. God despises double minded people but loves those that keep His commandments. Christian's can only move mountains, and command any mountains the devil has orchestrated to impede their progress to be thrown into the sea by faith and it will be established. This is the reason why the devil tries to put fears and uncertainty in the hearts of Christian's so as to diminish and undermine their authority in Christ.

Besides, the devil understand that when Christian's know their authority in Christ, they will no longer be infants that are toss to and fro by the waves, and are blown here and there by every wind of teaching, and by the cunning and craftiness of men in their fraudulent schemes. Christians should admonish all things as well as determine their stand and refuse to compromise their spiritual standard in Christ. This is the reason why the devil attacks Christian's with fear so that he can get them to compromise their stand in Christ. Christian's should not allow the devil to cause them to compromise their faith and stand in Christ because this could result to truncating their divine providence in Christ.

Therefore, Christian's cannot afford to miss out or lose out in the glorious future that God has predestined for them right before the foundation of the world because other people destines are connected to ours. If we truncate our destiny by walking and living in fear it means that destines connected to us will as well suffer loss. Therefore, Christian's

> *"If we truncate our destiny by walking and living in fear it means that destines connected to us will as well suffer loss".*

should be extremely careful not to let fear to control their hearts and minds and deprives them of launching out into the deep where God's purpose awaits them. God has made provisions and resources for us all, but for Christian's to access their divine provisions requires them to be obedient to God's divine call for their live. Consequently, Christians should also learn to say no to the devil's schemes such as fear, and instead they should adopt the glorious future that is ahead of them.

Chapter 4 – Separation from God

The devil's strategy is to promote enmity between God and His beloved children. The scripture says: *"you [are like] unfaithful wives [having illicit love affairs with the world and breaking your marriage vow to God]! Do you not know that being the world's friend is being God's enemy? So whoever chooses to be a friend of the world takes his stand as an enemy of God"*[45]. The devil uses different strategies and strongholds to try and capture the hearts and minds of Christian's. Therefore, Christian's should be disciplined and vigilant at all times because the devil (your adversary) roams about like a lion seeking whom he may devour. The devil's plan is to undermine

> *"Christians separate from God, when they walk in disobedience to God's commandments. Thus, they give the devil a foothold to hunt their lives".*

the faith of Christian's by causing God's children to walk in disobedience. Christians separate from God, when they walk in disobedience to God's commandments. Thus, they give the devil a foothold to haunt their lives. The Bible says that it is difficult to please God without faith, and faith is simultaneous to obedience. Fear forms the path by which the enemy may come and torment us. The Bible says that: *"fear has torment"*[46]

---

[45] James 4:4 AMP
[46] John 4:18 AKJV

and *"whosoever breaks the hedge the serpent will bite him"*[47]. Christian's breaks their hedge with God by walking in disobedience to God's instructions and mandates for their lives. Another thing to understand is that we have not received the spirit that will enslave us to fear, but have received the spirit of sonship, wherein we cry Abba Father. Also, *"for God did not give us a spirit of timidity (of cowardice, of craven and cringing and fawning fear), but [He has given us a spirit] of power and of love and of calm and well-balanced mind and discipline and self-control"*[48]. The devil strategic plan is to get Christian's away from God's protection; thus, Christians walk out of God's divine purpose for their lives.

Devil's Tactics 1 – Spirit of Disobedience

Disobedience is a spirit of the devil and must be cast out. If not, it will deprive us of fellowshipping with God. Disobedience will prompt us to rebel against God. The scripture says: *"for rebellion is as the sin of witchcraft, and stubbornness is as idolatry and teraphim (household good luck images). Because you have rejected the word of the Lord, He also has rejected you from being king"*[49]. Disobedience is a sin, and this is one of the ways that the devil uses to deny Christian's from entering their rest. Christian's that are willing and obedient will eat the good of the land. The devil does not want Christian's to eat the good of the land. The devil ensures that he ensnares God's children and fights them so that they can disobey God, hence; miss their good treasures in Christ.

For instance, many heroes' of faith started great, but when the devil captured their heart through disobedience they were discarded by God. Therefore, they did not make it to their promised land. Others, by His grace where given another chance. For example, in the case of King Saul;

---

[47] Ecclesiastes 10:8 AKJV
[48] 2 Timothy 1:7 AMP
[49] 1 Samuel 15:23 AMP

God asked him *"go and smite Amalek and utterly destroy all they have; do not spare them, but kill both man and woman, infant and suckling, ox and sheep, camel and donkey"*[50]. But King Saul disobeyed God: *"Saul smote the Amalekites from Havilah as far as Shur, which is east of Egypt. And he took Agag king of the Amalekites alive, though he utterly destroyed all the rest of the people with the sword. Saul and the people spared Agag and the best of the sheep, oxen, fatlings, lambs, and all that was good, and would not utterly destroy them; but all that was undesirable or worthless they destroyed utterly"*[51]. King Saul disobeyed God because he allowed the pleasures, delights, false glamour *and* deceitfulness of riches to stifle the instructions given to him by God.

The Bible warns Christian's not to be lovers of money, greedy for wealth and eager to obtain it by dubious means. This is because people who want to get rich, fall into diverse temptation and deception of the enemy and into many foolish and harmful desires that plunge men into ruin and destruction. The love of money is indeed the root of all kinds of evil.

> *"Many Christian's like King Saul have compromised their genuine salvation in Christ because of worldly popularity".*

Some people that are eager for money have wondered from their faith and have pierced themselves with many grieve. King Saul forfeited his divine call as a king of Israel for materialism purposes. In fact, he was more obsessed in acquiring more worldly things. Many Christian's like King Saul have compromised their genuine salvation in Christ because of worldly popularity. Surely, these are all set traps from the enemy in order to entrap God's children from fulfilling purpose.

The following case study is Moses. Moses was one of God's heroes of faith who was well-known for walking with God. He encountered God,

---

[50] 1 Samuel 15:3 AMP
[51] 1 Samuel 15:7-9 AMP

by fellowshipping in His presence. Moses encountered God, but it is difficult to believe that he could truncate his destiny. For example, the devil tried to frustrate Moses, in order to forfeit his race, but failed. He even went to the extent of using Moses' siblings against him, but God dealt with his siblings. The devil failed to get Moses through his siblings like in the case of Joseph in Genesis 37. However, the devil gained

> *"Brethren any weakness we fail to expose and bring correction to will indubitably be used against us by the devil to mark our downfall".*

an advantage in the life of Moses through his weakness. For example, Moses failed to work on his weakness called anger. This gave the devil a foothold in his life by dethroning him when he was at the mountain top heading for glory. Had it been that Moses worked on his anger, at his early stage of his ministry perhaps Moses could have made it to the promised land. For instance, Moses' desire to fast-forward his fate by killing the Egyptians landed him to the wilderness for 40 years. God later reactivated his destiny when He heard the cry of the Israelite and remembered the promise He made to the forefathers of Israel.

God gave Moses several opportunities to deal with his anger; he refused to work on it, thereby, burying it within himself. Moses decided to cover his weakness rather than bring an amendment to it. The devil then

> *"Brethren, it is essential that whilst we are still going through Jesus' training school that we aspire to bring correction or even allow God to mould us by turning our clutter into a message*

decided to attack him through his weakness. Brethren, any weakness we fail to expose, and bring correction to will indubitably be used against us by the devil to mark our downfall. Moses was a terror in the kingdom of darkness because of his strong relationship with God. The devil had been planning his destruction. Moses' mistake was that he refused to wait on God's appointed time but was reckless in his decisions; thus, his own self-will landed him in exile. This is what happen when we take decisions and matter in our own hands; rather than trust and wait for God's appointed time. Moses had to run for his life because the whole world wanted to terminate his life. Moses should have brought correction to his anger because it was his anger that pushed him to kill the Egyptians in the first instance. Brethren, it is essential that whilst we are still going through Jesus' training school that we aspire to bring correction or even allow God to mould us by turning our clutter into a message.

It is also essential that we deal with our past mistakes, hurts, misunderstandings, and misfortune so that we will not be deprived of running the race that God has preordained for us. This is because it may disqualify us, from entering our rest. For instance, in the case of Moses *"the Lord said to Moses, Take the rod, and assemble the congregation, you and Aaron your brother, and tell the rock before their eyes to give forth its water, and you shall bring forth to them water out of the rock; so you shall give the congregation and their*

> "Christian's should deal with their past mistake, hurts, misunderstandings, and misfortune so that it would not deprive us from running the race".

livestock drink. So Moses took the rod from before the Lord, as He commanded him. And Moses and Aaron assembled the congregation before the rock, and Moses said to them, Hear now, you rebels; must we bring you water out of this rock? And Moses lifted up his hand and with his rod he smote the rock [a] twice. And the water came out abundantly, and the congregation drank, and their livestock"[52].

Anger is a sin, and also a killer of destiny because it deprived Moses of his destiny. It was anger that caused Moses to smoke the rock twice when he was asked by God, "tell the rock before their eyes to give forth its water, and you shall bring forth to them water out of the rock". Moses gave in

---

52 Numbers 20:7-11 AMP

to the devil by acting in disobedience. I am sure that the devil was celebrating for getting Moses to miss the mark of his high calling. Walking with God is very demanding, costly and difficult because our responsibility increases when we become God's chosen vessels. Likewise, it is easier for us to fall because we are a victim in the kingdom of darkness. Moses opened the door for the enemy to come into his life through anger. Thus, Moses was disqualified from running the race because of his disobedience. God is not interested in how we start our

> *"God is not interested in how we start our race but how well and strong we finish it. This is because many can start the race but not everybody has the knack of finishing their race, and get to their divine destination".*

race but how well and strong we finish it. This is because many start the race, but not everybody has the knack of finishing their race, and get to their divine destination. In the case of Moses, he did start the race, but was later disqualified, thereby, missed the mark. Brethren, of what use is it to start a race; but towards the end of your race be rendered disqualified. It is better we don't start than start and cannot finish well and strong.

Jonah is another Bible character that disobeyed God. God asked him to rise and go to Nineveh, that great city, to proclaim against it. For the wickedness had come up before Him. Jonah acted as though he was deaf to God's instructions. Hence, he wanted to escape from God to Tarshish. Jonah was running away from being a prophet of the Most High

> *"Brethren, of what use is it to start a race; but towards the end of your race be rendered disqualified. It is better you don't start than start and cannot finish well and strong".*

God. Jonah determined in his mind, to flee from God's presence by paying for his trip to Tarshish. Christian's should not assume that they can abscond from God who made heaven and earth. As the scripture says "if I ascend up into heaven, thou art there: If I take the wings of the morning, and dwell in the uttermost parts of the sea; even there shall thy hands lead me, and thy right hand shall hold me"[53]. How can we run away from the spirit of God? In fact, how can we run away from His presence? Jonah thought that he had escaped from God but little did he know this same God had orchestrated a plan to trap him. The Lord did this by causing a great turbulence and outrage of

> *"God sometimes permits the storms of life to come against His children just to get their attention".*

violence upon the sea; thus, the ship would have being broken. It was because of Jonah that God sent the storm against the ship. In Jonah case, God had mercy on him compared to the rest of the Bible characters. Brethren, the storm you are facing now in your life could be because you tried to run away from God's calling for your life. Thus, God sometimes uses storms to redirect His children back to their divine purpose. Indisputably, we might even be in a situation whereby despite all we have laboured to work for seems to come to fruitless efforts and shambles. This could be because we are trying to run away from God like Jonah. God sometimes permits the storms of life to come against His children just to get our attention.

The mariners became afraid because of the raging storms, and decided to wake Jonah from sleep so that they can call on his God. How can Jonah now have the boldness to call on this same God he pretended to have been deaf to His instructions? Jonah

> *"God often uses other people's disobedience to bring others to Christ".*

was not in right standing with God the moment he disobeyed God's instructions. The mariners decided that they will cast lots and whomsoever the lot falls upon would be intensely interrogated. Of

---

53 Psalms 139:8-10 KJV

course, the lots fell on Jonah; this resulted to intense questioning. The mariners asked Jonah questions such as his occupation, where he was coming from, his initial country and nationality. The mariners where aware that Jonah was running away from God's call as a prophet; hence, Jonah confessed to the mariners that he was the cause of their problem. The mariners feared that Jonah might be killed when he asked them to throw him into the sea. For example, they tried all they could to prevent the ragging of the sea; but rather the sea became more hostile towards them. The mariners then asked God for mercy not to be accounted for Jonah's life; before they took Jonah and cast him into the sea. The Bible recorded that immediately they did that the sea ceased from ragging. Thus, Jonah disobedience to God caused the mariners to fear and worship Jonah's God; thus, made a vow to God. God often uses other people's disobedience to lead others to Christ.

The aftermath of disobedience could be extremely disastrous. It is better to be for God; than to be against God. This is because we cannot stand the chance to survive God's wrath and judgement. As a result of Jonah disobedience, the Lord caused a great fish to swallow Jonah. Jonah was in the belly of the fish for

> *"Many Christians want God to rough handle them before they come to surrender to Him".*

three days and nights. Jonah was lucky because he had a second chance from God. God had to break Jonah in the midst of the storms just to teach him a lesson of obedience. Jonah encountered God whilst he was in the belly of the fish and this led to his repentance and restoration. Many Christians want God to rough handle them before they come to surrender to Him. Obedience is better than sacrifice; it is better to obey God, wholeheartedly than be broken by God like Jonah. God's chastisements are not grievous, but when we willingly surrender to Him, He gives us the grace to bear His chastisement because of His sufficient grace upon our life.

Brethren, the Lord has the power over the fishes and the fowls of the earth. For example, God in His infinite mercy prevented the fish from consuming Jonah. As a result, Jonah became a burden to the fish in his stomach. The fish would have regretted finding Jonah because God had a seal on Him written *"Touch not"*. When God, was through with Jonah chastisement He then spoke to the fish to release Jonah. For example, the fish vomited Jonah by taking him to Nineveh, the same city he was running away from. In

> *"Not every Christian will have a second chance like Jonah"*.

the case of Jonah, God was merciful unto him, thereby granting him a second chance. He later ceased that opportunity and obeyed God. In fact, he learnt his lessons the hard way. Not every Christian will receive a second chance like Jonah. Therefore, whatever God asks us to do just ensure that we follow Him to the latter. Even when we cannot trace Him, because there is no searching of His understanding; His knowledge is infinite.

Christian's should also endeavour to see that they work on their weakness or anything that will act as hindrances to their future glory and joy. It is better we deal with our past now before it is too late. Dealing with your past is vital because if not done it could open the door of your life to the enemy for him to torment you. Thus, it might cause you to miss the mark of your high calling like in the case of Moses.

Devil Tactics 2 – Spiritual Deadness

The consequences attributed to disobedience are that it results to spiritually deadness. Spiritual deadness results from allowing your flesh to control your spirit man. As the scripture says *"for those who are according to the flesh and are controlled by its unholy desires set their minds on and [d]pursue those things which gratify the flesh, but those who are according to the Spirit and are controlled by the desires of the Spirit set their minds on and* [e]*seek those things which gratify the [Holy] Spirit. Now the mind of the flesh [which is sense and reason without the Holy Spirit] is death [death that* [f]*comprises all the miseries arising from sin, both here and hereafter]. But the mind of the [Holy] Spirit is life and [soul] peace [both now and forever]. [That is] because the mind of the flesh [with its carnal thoughts and purposes] is hostile to God, for it does not submit itself to God's Law; indeed it cannot. So then those who are living the life of the flesh [catering to the appetites and impulses of their carnal nature] cannot please or satisfy God, or be acceptable to Him. But you are not living the life of the flesh, you are living the life of the Spirit, if the [Holy] Spirit of God [really] dwells within you [directs and controls you]. But if anyone does not possess the [Holy] Spirit of Christ, he is none of His [he does not belong to Christ, is not truly a child of God]. But if Christ lives in you, [then although] your [natural] body is dead by reason of sin and guilt, the spirit is alive because of [the] righteousness [that He imputes to you]. And if the Spirit of Him Who raised up Jesus from the dead dwells in you, [then] He Who raised up Christ Jesus from the dead will also restore to life your mortal (short-lived, perishable) bodies through His Spirit Who dwells in you. So then, brethren, we are debtors, but not to the flesh [we are not obligated to our carnal nature], to live [a life ruled by the standards set up by the dictates] of the flesh. For if you live according to [the dictates of] the flesh, you will surely die. But if through the power of the [Holy] Spirit you are [habitually] putting to death (making extinct, deadening) the [evil] deeds prompted by the body, you shall [really and genuinely] live forever. For all who are led by the Spirit of God are sons of God. For [the Spirit which] you have now received [is] not a spirit of slavery to put you once more in bondage to fear, but you have received the Spirit of adoption [the Spirit producing sonship] in [the bliss of] which we cry, Abba (Father)! Father! The Spirit Himself [thus] testifies together with our own spirit, [assuring us] that we are children of God*[54].

---

[54] Romans 8:5-16 AMP

The handiwork of the devil is to cause Christian's to walk in the flesh thereby fulfilling the desires and lust of the flesh in the expense of their genuine salvation in Christ. The devil causes Christian's to pursue the lustfulness of the flesh in order to satiate their hunger and satanic taste. *"Satan, who is the god of this world, has blinded the minds of those who don't believe. They are unable to see the glorious light of the Good News. They don't understand this message about the glory of Christ, who is the exact likeness of God"*[55]. The devil's desire is to truncate the destinies of God's children. Thus, he uses his fake powers to prevent the hearts and minds of God's children from believing the truth about the word of God. Spiritual deadness also derives from a carnal mind and a carnal mind denotes from the works and doings of the devil. The devil fights Christian's in their flesh in order to deprive them of their heavenly inheritance and spiritual blessings. The Bible says that: *"now the mind of the flesh [which is sense and reason without the Holy Spirit] is death [death that* [f]*comprises all the miseries arising from sin, both here and hereafter]*[56]. When a Christian is spiritually dead, he ceases from receiving spiritual signals from God. This means that his spiritual antenna is disjointed from God. The outcome thereafter is that he is unable to hear and recognise the voice of God because the devil has hijacked his spiritual connectivity with God. It is dangerous to be in a position whereby we are alive physically but dead spiritually.

> "The handiwork of the devil is to cause Christian's to walk in the flesh thereby fulfilling the desires and the lust of the flesh in the expense of their genuine salvation in Christ in order to satiate their hunger and satanic taste".

> "When a Christian is spiritually dead, he cease from receiving spiritual signals from God. This means that his spiritual antenna is disjointed from God".

---

55 2 Corinthians 4:4 NLT
56 Romans 8:6a AMP

Spiritual death separates us from God because we no longer dictate His presence and obey His instructions because we are toss to and fro. Thus, the fear of the unknown has taken a grip on us; hence, result to doubt and unbelief. If you live by the dictates of the flesh, we must surely die. This is as a result of living in the flesh, and by our appetites and impulses we cannot please God and be acceptable to Him.

Furthermore, to be dead spiritually causes humanity to lose connection with the Most High God, and this leads to an unfulfilled destiny. Also, we are likely to sin against God by missing the mark. Missing the mark means to be separated from God. The Bible says that: *"for the wages of sin is death, but the free gift of God is eternal life through Christ Jesus our Lord"*[57]. The scripture also says: *"whatsoever is not of faith is sin"*[58]. Therefore, is a sin to doubt God and His word. For example, the Bible says that it is impossible to please God without faith because if we come to Him we must believe that He is and also a rewarder of them that diligently seek Him. The devil wants us to be dead both physically and spiritually. Christian's should always be alert and vigilant of the enemies' deceits.

Cure for Spiritual Death

The cure for spiritual death is to become spiritually awakened. Christian's should be prepared to live according to the spirit of God. This is because if Christ' spirit resides within us; it will direct and control (subdue) our flesh and its lustful desires. If Christ resides in us, He causes our natural body to be dead by reason of sin and guilt. Thereby, He makes His spirit alive within us because of His righteousness that is imputed in us. Also, the spirit of God; will cause us to overcome our carnal and Adamic nature. This is because that spirit that raises Jesus from the dead resides

---

[57] Romans 6:23 NLT
[58] Romans 14:23 ASV

in us; it will quicken our mortal body. Many that are led by the spirit of God are the sons of God. The spirit of God in us enables us to renew and transform our thought pattern. Certainty, it brings freedom and liberation from the devil's strongholds. God's spirit cleanses us from all impurities and idols that we may have exalted above God.

Baptism of the Holy Spirit

The spirit is known as the water of repentance. Jesus Christ baptises us with the Holy Spirit and with fire. The requirement of entering into the kingdom of God is to be born of water and of the spirit. The Holy Spirit also cleanses us and watches us through His word. The same spirit which is the spirit of God saves us and causes us to live a holy life that is pleasing and acceptable to God. The water symbolizes baptism of the Holy Spirit. The functions of the water are to consecrate us and also present us blameless before God. Christian's are saved by the redemption power of our Lord Jesus Christ. Therefore, Christians should seek to draw near to God with a sincere heart in full assurance of their faith, having our hearts sprinkled to cleanse us from a guilty conscience and our bodies washed with pure water.

Devil Tactics 3 – Friendship with the World

Christian's that are spiritually dead, automatically become friends with the world. This is one aspect the devil uses to impede God's children from walking in obedience to God's will for their lives. Friendship with the world is enmity with God. The Bible urges Christian's to stop loving the world and the things that are in the world. If anyone persists in loving the world, the Father's love is not in him. Christian's are advised not to conform to the patterns of this world, but to be transformed by renewing their mind. By doing so, they are then able to test and approve what God's will is i.e. His good, pleasing and perfect will. It is needful that Christian's resist any temptation that comes their way. For example, if Jesus could resist the devil when he took Him to a very high mountain and showed Him all the kingdoms of the world and their splendour, and said to Jesus all these I give to you when you fall down and worship me. Jesus answered, get thee hence, Satan: for it is written that you shall only worship your Lord your God; and Him only shall you serve. This means that if Jesus was tempted by the devil, we His followers are assured that the devil would also tempt us with the splendours of the world so that we lose our focus and trust in our Sovereign God. In addition, Jesus Christ was victorious over the devil, thus; Christian's should be rest assured that they too would be victorious over the wiles of the devil. All God's children have to do is to stand their ground and tell the devil to get thee behind me.

The world offers only a craving for physical pleasure, a craving for everything we see, and pride in our achievements and possessions. These are not from God but from the world. Christian's should seek to clothe themselves with the spirit of our Lord Jesus Christ, and refrain from gratifying the desires of their sinful nature. The Bible says that all the boasting we brag about are all evil. This is because the spirit that resides in us lust after envy and this

> *"The world offers only a craving for physical pleasure, a craving for everything we see, and pride in our achievements and possessions. These are not from God but from the world."*

is also the reason why God resists the proud and gives grace to the humble. Therefore, Christian's are to submit totally to God; resist the devil, and he will flee from us. The Bible says that death, and destructions are never satisfied neither are the eyes of men. Christian's sinful nature war against their soul; i.e. to take us out of the presence and fellowship of God. For instance, it was the desire for physical recreation and materialism that caused Eve to fall prey to the devil's tactics. The Bible says that Eve saw that the fruits of the trees were good for food and also pleasing to the eyes. The food was also desirable for gaining wisdom; that is why she partook of it and also lured her husband to sin. Adam and Eve inability to resist the devil's satanic schemes gave him the legal right against God's children.

On the other hand, Peter tried to reprimand Jesus from paying his price of His high calling. Jesus' price was to be killed and raised back to life by going to Jerusalem to suffer many things in the hands of the elders, chief priest and teachers of the law. For instance, Jesus told Peter to *"get thee behind me Satan"*! Jesus Christ response was that he was a stumbling block to Him because you do not have in mind the things of God, but the things of men. This is what the devil wants from the unset; his intension is to cause God's children to walk in disobedience so that he could have access to their personal lives. Walking in disobedience gives the devil a foothold in the lives of Christian's. However, walking in obedience to God's instructions shields Christians from the devil's tactics. As the scripture says that: *"for the god of this world has blinded the unbelievers' minds [that they should not discern the truth], preventing them from seeing the illuminating light of the Gospel of the glory of Christ (the Messiah), who is the Image and Likeness of God"*[59]. The devil obtained the keys of this world because of Adam and Eve's disobedience to God. Jesus Christ had to come and pay the price to redeem mankind from the wiles of the devil and also to take back the keys that Adam and Eve sabotaged. God redeemed us from the curse of the law being made a curse for us. God made Jesus who had no sin to be sin for us, so that in Him we might become the righteousness of God. In order to redeem those under the law, that we might receive the full rights of sonship. Jesus' death paid for our transgressions as well as redeemed us from the snares of the devil. Therefore, Christian's should aim to glorify God both in their body and in their spirit because we are gods.

---

[59] 2 Corinthians 4:4 AMP

Christian's should not be obsessed with accumulating materialistic things, because if we do so it means that we are not content with what we have. The scripture says: godliness and contentment is great gain. God has promised not to leave us or forsake us. Christians turn away from God and become friends with the world because of the love of money and not being content with what they have. The disadvantage of chasing after worldly fame and recognitions is that it disconnects us from God and makes us a friend with the world. Worldly fame and recognition denies us access to God and His benefits. Friendship with the world and its pleasures turns out to become an enemy with God.

> "Worldly fame and recognition denies us access to God and His benefits. Friendship with the world and its pleasures turns out to become an enemy with God."

This acts as a stumbling block in receiving God's promises and fellowshipping with Him. For example, the devil has made God's children so busy with work that they hardly ever spend time with God in His presence. Christian's are deceived by the devil because they have allowed the love of money and materialism to cloud and starve their faith in God. Therefore, Christians no longer have faith in God because they rely on their own efforts, in order to obtain their worldly achievements.

If we have faith like a mustard seed we can command the mountains in our life to get out, and be thrown into the sea, and it will be done. Christians can do terrible things in righteous because the serve a God of impossibilities. However, the problem is that Christian's have allowed the cares of the world to starve their faith in Christ. Christian's faith in God reduces when they allow the worries of life such as paying bills, feeding and catering for their family to deprive them from encountering God. As a result, Christians strive to work hard to make ends meet instead of trusting in God. The devil strategic plan is to bring demarcation between God and His children.

Mandates for rekindling your fire for God

Christian's should endeavour to turn their hearts towards God statues and not towards their own selfish gain. They should also refrain from been obsessed with accumulating material wealth, but rather they should ask for God's wisdom so that they can show restraint. Christians should be wise not to store up treasures here on earth because it is likely to perish or be stolen. It is essential to store up treasures in heaven, where it is impossible for the devil to break in and steal. Every vessel of God should refrain from greediness and all kinds of immorality such as been lovers of money. Christian's should therefore, strive to put to death all that belongs to this human nature such as sexual immoralities, impurities, lust, evil desires and greed, which is idolatry.

The Bible says that a greedy man stirs up dissensions, but he who trusts in the Lord will prosper. It is better to have a little, and have the fear of the Lord, than have great wealth with turmoil. Certainly, the devil's strategic plan is to foster great turmoil in the lives of Christian's. He does that by making Christian's desire worldly popularity in the expense of God and His word. Therefore, Christian's should be vigilant and be on guard against all kinds of greed because a man's life does not consist in the abundance of his possessions. Like the case of the rich man who had many possessions but lack the room to store his crops. He later thought to himself saying: he will destroy his barn and build a bigger one so that he will be able to store his grains and goods. His soul was required of him, because he lays up treasures for himself and is not rich towards God. Certainly, the treasures of wickedness profit nothing.

The rich man had the opportunity to be a blessing to others such as the poor around him, but he refused because he was consumed by his own selfish gains. For example, the Bible warns us not to boast about tomorrow for we do not know what tomorrow will hold. The rich man boasted about tomorrow by failing to trust in God, but he relied on himself. Thus, he destroyed his former barn in order to build a bigger one so that there would be more rooms to store his goods and gains. God is the only one that can determine what tomorrow holds and not man. As a result, humanity are required to align themselves to God's will for their lives. Additionally, the fact that we are alive today is to the glory of God. Christian's should therefore bear in mind that on judgement day, they will be liable to God for their works here on earth. Of what use is it to live your life outside of God's purpose and on the day of judgement be disqualified from running your race. Indeed, what does it profits a man to gain the whole world and then lose his soul in the kingdom of heaven?

It is essential to note that Christian's are living a wasted life when they are rich in worldly things and not in God. Christian's who want to get rich often fall into temptations and traps of the enemy; and into many foolish and harmful desires that plunge them into ruin and destructions. The man that pretends to be rich has nothing, but the one that pretends to be poor has great wealth. God also chooses the poor in the eyes of the world, to be rich in faith, and to inherit the kingdom of God. For instance, the Bible

> "Christian's are living a wasted life when they are rich in worldly things and not in God. Christian's who want to get rich often fall into temptations and traps of the enemy; and into many foolish and harmful desires that plunges them into ruin and destructions".

says that the rich man went away sorrowful when asked to sell his possessions and give to the poor because he had great possessions. Jesus told His disciples that it will be difficult for those who possess great wealth, and refuses to discard it to enter the kingdom of God. The lesson here is that whenever we come to God; Christian's have to sell and discard all for Him like Paul. You may be wondering why? It is because we cannot serve two masters at the same time. We cannot serve both God and money (i.e. devil).

Christian's should know that this world is fading away, along with everything that people crave. But anyone who does what pleases God's will live forever. Therefore, Christian's should be careful not to involve themselves with the things of the world because the world is passing away. Christian's drift from their faith in God into becoming friends with this world, because they allow their shortcoming to darken and conceal their faith and belief system in God. They crave for the wealth of unbelievers thereby, allowing their desire for physical pleasure and the deceitfulness of worldly riches to separate them from God. Christian's have allowed the worries of life, the deceitfulness of wealth and the desires of other things to come into their lives, thereby choking God's word in them and rendering it unfruitful.

It is necessary for Christian's to note that: *"no soldier in active service entangles himself in the affairs of everyday life, so that he may please the one who enlisted him as a solider"*[60]. It is for freedom that Christ set us free in the first instance. Therefore, Christian's should stand firm and not allow themselves to be burdened again by the yoke of slavery. Christian's have escaped the corruption of this world through the knowledge of our Lord and Saviour Jesus Christ. If they are entangled in it again, they are worse off at the end than they were at the beginning. For we live by faith and not by sight. Thus, Christian's should not be consumed by their present troubles, but rather fix their gaze on things they cannot see. The things we see now will soon fade away, but the things that we cannot see will last forever. For by this hope we were saved. But hope that is seen is no hope at all. Who hopes for what he already has?

We are hedged in (pressed) on every side [troubled and oppressed in every way], but not cramped or crushed; we suffer embarrassments and are perplexed and unable to find a way out, but not driven to despair; we are pursued (persecuted and hard driven), but not deserted [to stand alone]; we

---

60 2 Timothy 2:4 NASB

are struck down to the ground, but never struck out and destroyed; Always carrying about in the body the liability and exposure to the same putting to death that the Lord Jesus suffered, so that the [[a]resurrection] life of Jesus also may be shown forth by and in our bodies. For we who live are constantly [experiencing] being handed over to death for Jesus' sake, that the [[b]resurrection] life of Jesus also may be evidenced through our flesh which is liable to death. Thus death is actively at work in us, but [it is in order that [c]our] life [may be actively at work] in you. Yet we have the same spirit of faith as he had who wrote, I have believed, and therefore have I spoken. We too believe, and therefore we speak, assured that He who raised up the Lord Jesus will raise us up also with Jesus and bring us [along] with you into His presence. For all [these] things are [taking place] for your sake, so that the more grace (divine favour and spiritual blessing) extends to more and more people and multiplies through the many, the more thanksgiving may increase [and redound] to the glory of God. Therefore we do not become discouraged (utterly spiritless, exhausted, and wearied out through fear). Though our outer man is [progressively] decaying and wasting away, yet our inner self is being [progressively] renewed day after day. For our light, momentary affliction (this slight distress of the passing hour) is ever more and more abundantly preparing and producing and achieving for us an everlasting weight of glory [beyond all measure, excessively surpassing all comparisons and all calculations, a vast and transcendent glory and blessedness never to cease!], Since we consider and look not to the things that are seen but to the things that are unseen; for the things that are visible are temporal (brief and fleeting), but the things that are invisible are deathless and everlasting[61]. The fact that you are down now does not mean that God has forsaken or abandoned you. This is another aspect that the devil is using to capture God's children; especially during their waiting period. The devil causes their hearts and minds to faint; so that Christian's starts

---

[61] 2 Corinthians 4:8-18 AMP

to lose perspective and trust in God. Thereby, Christian's are forced to seek other alternatives by running after worldly pleasures and this leads to Christian's compromising their faith in God.

Godly Counsel

Christian's should set their minds on things above, not on earthly things. Setting your minds on earthly things causes the destinies of Christian's to be truncated. This is because they have made their god their stomach, and their glory is in their shame. Our citizenship is in heaven, and we wait earnestly for our Saviour the Lord Jesus Christ. Christian's are in this world, but not of the world; hence, they should be of good cheers even if the encounter great tribulation as a result of their faith. One thing God assures His children is that we would overcome because Jesus Christ overcame this world. Surely, Christian's are hated by the world because

> *"Christian's are hated by the world because they have refused to undermine God's standards. Hence, they should prepare themselves to suffer for Christ's sake."*

they have refused to undermine God's standards. Hence, they should prepare themselves to suffer for Christ's sake. There is an assurance in God's word, that whosoever is born of God overcomes the world, because therein their victory lies in their faith in God. Christian's should not allow their carnal desires to deprive them of walking in God's spirit because the final result is very inauspicious. Rather Christian's should strive to follow God's footsteps and also walk in obedience to His will and instructions. Furthermore, Christian's should be prepared to put aside every weight that will stop them from running their race. Besides, Christian's should also be willing to say no to the wiles of the devil by resisting him constantly, and he will flee from us.

Devil Tactics 4 – The Spirit of Unforgiveness

The spirit of unforgiveness is one of the ways that the devil gains an advantage into the lives of Christians. The disadvantage to this is that it prevents our prayers from being answered by God. The devil's plan is to thwart God's children from entering their rest. For example, the Bible says that if we are offering a gift at the altar of God; and it appears that we are not in good terms with our brother; then leave your gifts at the altar and go and reconcile with your brother, then come and offer your gift. Unforgiveness is a sin and

> *"The spirit of unforgiveness is one of the ways that the devil gains an advantage into the lives of Christians. The disadvantage to this is that it prevents our prayers from being answered by God".*

God does not accept the gifts of a sinner because he is too holy to behold iniquity. The Bible urges Christian's to live at peace with all men and that they should not repay anyone evil for evil. Instead, they should be careful to do what is right in the eyes of all men.

Peter asked Jesus how many times he should forgive his brother when he sin against him. Up to seven times? Jesus' response to Peter was not seven times, but seventy-times seven. Brethren, even if your friend does something to hurt your feelings; it is essential that you let him know his faults rather than announcing it publicly. This is because you are likely to win him back to Jesus Christ through your actions. For example, if your brother continues to hurt your feelings and keep coming back to repent; just accept him and pray for his salvation in the Lord. Failing to forgive your loved ones of their wrong gives the devil a foothold over your life and destiny.

The kingdom of God is like a king who wants to settle accounts with his servants. Whilst he was accounting for his debtors a man who owed him ten thousand talents were brought to him, and since they were unable to pay, the captain ordered their belongings to be sold to recover his and his family debts. But the servants fell on their knees and begged the account manager to be patient with him, and he would pay him everything. The servant master had mercy on him and cancelled all his debts. But this same servant that received forgiveness from his superior commander refused to cancel the debts of his junior servant. Rather he rendered justices without mercy by locking him up in prison until he paid all he owes. When the other servants saw the unforgiving spirit in his master heart, he was greatly distressed, and he ran to report it to the head of his master, by telling him everything that his master did. The master called the servant in and queried his actions saying, you wicked servant you asked for forgiveness and I forgave all your debts, but you have also refused to forgive the debts of your junior servant. His master was so upset and asked him; should not he have mercy on his junior servant? The master handed him over to the prison guards to be tortured until he paid all his debts.

The example above helps us to understand that we reap what we sow. For instance, if we sow good seeds, we will reap good seeds in return. But if we sow evil seeds, we will reap evil seeds in return. The first master forgave his servant of his debts but his servant refused to forgive his junior servant; hence, his debts were reinstated. The devil's plan is to deprive Christian's from their true inheritances and blessing from God. The Bible says blessed are the merciful for they shall obtain mercy. The devil also uses the spirit of unforgiveness in order to gain access into the lives of Christian's. Therefore, Christian's should pray and ask God to give them the grace to forgive their debtors and those that have crushed their spirit.

God intends that Christian's live in harmony with their fellow brethren. It is also the desire of God for us to love and forgive others as He had loved and forgiven us of our trespasses. This is because whoever conceals their sins will not prosper but if they profess and forsake it they are guaranteed to obtain God's mercy. For instance, it is difficult to love those who have severely damaged your feelings; but the grace of God is sufficient for you. Just ask Him because His strength is made perfect in your weakness. There is a motto that says *"to err is human and to forgive divine"*. No one is above mistakes, and this also includes fellow Christian's. Both Christians and none Christians will always fall short by stepping on your toes, but as Christian's, we should try to forgive one another and also be determined to pay the price for the glory that awaits us.

Cure for Unforgiveness

The cure for unforgiveness is to daily work out our own salvation with fear and trembling. In the process of aspiring to work out your salvation with fear and trembling; Christian's should aim to eschew anything that will serve as a hindrance to them making heaven. Unforgiveness is the work of the flesh because it comes with strife, envy and bitterness. Thus, we cannot make it to heaven if you manifest the spirit of unforgiveness. So Christian's should seek to guide their heart with all diligence because out of it flow the issues of life. The heart of a Christian is the wellspring of life, and it determines the course of your life. Therefore,

> *"Unforgiveness is the work of the flesh because it comes with strife, envy, and bitterness."*

Christian's cannot afford to give the devil a foothold by exhibiting the spirit of unforgiveness. The Bible says that it is the things that come out of a man that defiles a man. Hence, Christians are required to feed their spirit (i.e. our heart, soul and spirit) with the word of God. The Bible also says that the thing that comes out of your mouth comes from your heart and this make a man unclean. Out of the heart come evil thoughts, murder, adultery, sexual immoralities, theft, false testimonies and slander.

The good man brings forth good seeds stored in his heart, and the evil man brings evil seeds stored in his heart. Out of the abundance of the heart the mouth speaks. In other words, your speech is consumed by the fruits you have stored in your heart. Brethren should be cautious and careful not to allow what they encounter to seize their genuine salvation in the Lord. This is because the devil desires to fight us in order for us to denounce our Maker and serve him. Christian's should also listen to God because He helps us to make accurate decisions through His divine wisdom.

Chapter 5 – Stand your Ground

Christian's should not be ignorant of the devil's devices because the devil is trying to take advantage of Christian's in order to outsmart them. The devil is seeking various ways to render Christian's unfit for purpose. This is the reason why Christian's are constantly in the battlefield with the devil because he wants to gain a foothold in their lives. For instance, Simon would have fallen victim to the devil schemes because the devil desired to have Simon, in order that he may sift him to wheat. Jesus intervened and prayed for him that his faith will fail not and that after his converted that he should strengthen his brethren. One thing to note is that the devil is not happy to see God's children fulfil their purposes here on earth, because his kingdom will be invaded and his lawful captives will be delivered. Therefore, Christian's should be alert and disciplined because their enemy prowl around like a roaring lion seeking for whom to devour.

> *"The devil is seeking for various ways to render Christian's unfit for purpose. This is the reason why Christian's are constantly in the battlefield with the devil because he wants to gain a foothold in their lives."*

Indeed your struggle is not against flesh and blood, but against the rules, against the authorities, against the powers of this dark world and the spiritual forces of evil in the heavenly realms. Christian's should note that when running this race they should be prepared to sacrifice all because the price is given to the successful winner. This is because all athletes are discipline in their training; they do it to win a price that will fade away, but we do it for eternal prize. No wonder Satan masquerades himself as an angel of light. Therefore, in order to battle and compete with the devil will require us to go into strict training. Christian's will have to fight in order to finish the race and keep their faith. Also, Christian's should note that in order to receive the crown of victory as an athlete will require them to compete according to the rule. Christian's should not allow themselves to be entangled with anything that will stop them from running the race. Do not allow people who delight in false humility and the worship of angels disqualify you from receiving your heavenly reward. This is because such people are misleading and unspiritual. Christian's should aim to push toward the price of their high calling.

The Bible calls Christian's who persevere under trials blessed because they are faithful during trialling period. Thus, such Christians receive a crown of life that God has promised those who love Him. Jesus Christ has rescued us from the dominion of darkness and brought us into the kingdom of God. Likewise, we as Christian's should be prepared to turn the eyes, hearts and minds of people in darkness into light; and from the power of Satan into God. So that, they may receive forgiveness of sins and be sanctified and justified through faith. In order for Christian's to be successful in doing this; they have to put on all of God's armour so that they will be able to stand firm against all the strategies of the devil. Now is the time for Christian's to put away the deeds of darkness and put on the armour of light. Putting on the full armour of God enables Christian's to stand their ground against the wiles of the devil. Then after, the armour is worn they will have to submit to God, and when they do, then; when they resist the devil; the devil does not have a choice than to flee from us.

Putting on your whole armour

It is essential that Christian's put on their whole armour because in it lies the power to resist the devil. The armour of God enables Christian's to stand their ground against the enemy. For without the armour of God, Christian's are likely to be injured in the day of battle. The armour of God acts like a shield against

> *"The armour of God enables Christian's to stand their ground against the enemy. For without the armour of God Christian's are likely to be injured in the day of battle."*

the devil. For example, if Christian's fails to put on their whole amour they expose themselves to the devil and the arrows that flies by day. The whole armour of God cannot be overemphasized, but it is an essential weapon of warfare. Below are eight weapons of warfare or perhaps whole armour, that Christian's should be prepared to put on daily if they want victory over the devil.

Weapon of warfare 1 – Loins girt with Truth

Christian's need to put on their lions girt with truth in order to contend against flesh and blood, principalities, powers, rulers of darkness in this world and against spiritual wickedness in high places. Jesus Christ is this truth as the scripture says His the way, the truth and

> *"Christian's need to put on their loins girt with truth in order to contend against flesh and blood, principalities, powers, rulers of darkness in this world and against spiritual wickedness in high places."*

the life. No one comes to the Father except through Him. Likewise, Jesus Christ is the Word that became flesh and dwells among us. For we have seen His glory, the glory of the One and Only, who came from the Father, full of grace and truth. In fact, this same grace and truth came through Jesus Christ. He is known as the Resurrection, and the Life and those who believe in Him live because in Him was life and that life was the light of men. Also, Jesus Christ has come to give us insight in order to know Him who is true; even in His Son Jesus Christ because He is true God and eternal life. Besides because of Him, we have access to the Father by one spirit. Christian's were also able to gain access to the Father by faith, and we stand upon that same faith.

Knowing and understanding this truth will give us victory over the enemy especially when we are wrestling against flesh and blood and principalities and powers. This same truth we know will liberate us and set us free from sin and traps of the enemy. If Jesus Christ set us free, we are free indeed. This means that we have been set free from sin and have become a servant of righteousness. Knowing the fact that Christ was raised from the dead, and death no longer has dominion over Him. It gives us assurance and victory over the devil. We are buried with Him through

> "Knowing the truth that Christ was raised from the dead, and death no longer has dominion over Him gives us assurance and victory over the devil."

baptism into death in order that, just as Christ was raised from the dead through the glory of the Father, we also may live a new life. This means Jesus has paid the price for your sins, and sin does not have jurisdiction over us because we are not under the law but under grace. As a result, to this He now holds the keys of death and Hades.

The Lord is the Spirit, and where the Spirit of the Lord is, there is freedom. It is for this same freedom that Christ came to set us free; therefore, we need to stand and refuse to be yoked by slavery. This means that we should not use our freedom to indulge in a sinful nature but to serve each other in love. Knowing this truth is not enough to give us freedom over the devil, but Chris-

> "Knowing this truth is not enough to give us freedom over the devil but Christian's should be doers of the word because it is in the doing of the word that His blessing outpours on us."

tian's should be doers of the word because it is in the doing of the word that His blessing outpours on us. This freedom that God has given us should not be used to cover up evil but to be used as servants of the Most High God. Therefore, understanding this truth and the mysteries that lies beneath the word of God helps us to subdue the kingdom of darkness. For without the knowledge of the word of God, victory cannot be assured.

It is the truth we know that will overcome any situation that daily comes our way. Therefore, Christian's should strive to walk in truth and speak the truth always. The word of God is truth because Jesus Christ brought us forth by the word of truth. The word became flesh and dwells among us. God teaches His children through His word. In Him, we have heard the word of truth. The gospel of salvation, and by believing in Him we were sealed with the promise of the Holy Spirit who then teaches us our inheritance on how to obtain it and possess it. Christian's need to sanctify themselves in truth for His word is truth.

God also lead His children by the truth in His words and also teaches us; for He is the God of salvation. His word is also the light and the truth that leads us and brings us to His holy habitation. It is in this same truth that we gain an advantage over the devil. This is because when the Spirit of truth comes, He will guide us into all truth; for He will not speak of His own initiative, but whatever He hears His Father say, He will speak and reveal what is to come. Besides, God is a Spirit, and those who worship Him must worship in spirit and truth. Therefore, Christian's should aspire to be diligent to present themselves approved of God, as a workman who is not ashamed of the gospel but handles the word of truth accurately. Furthermore, Christian's should strive to speak the truth in love. It is in this loin girt about with truth that we are able to stand against all the schemes of the devil.

Weapon of Warfare 2 - Breastplate of righteousness

The breastplate of righteous shields us from the enemy attack when wrestling against the devil. Being righteous means having a right standing with God through faith; like Abraham who believed in God, and it was accounted to Him as righteous. Jesus Christ is the Lord of Righteousness. It was because of Him that we are united with Christ. He became for us wisdom from God – that is our righteousness, holiness and redemption. We are made righteous in God through Christ because Christ has made us righteous. It was by one man that sin and death reigned; likewise through Jesus Christ we are able to receive abundance of grace and the gifts of righteousness.

> *"The breastplate of righteous shields us from the enemy attack when wrestling against the devil."*

Therefore, there is no more condemnation for those that are in Christ Jesus because we belong to Him, the power of life-giving Spirit has freed us from the power of sin that leads to death. For this cause, we've been set free from sin, and have become servants to righteousness. This means that sin will no longer have power over us because we are not under the law but under grace. God has given His children great and precious promises to allow us to share in His divine nature, so that we may escape the world's corruption caused by evil desires. This means that according to His divine power, he has given us all things that pertain to life and godliness, through the knowledge of Him that has called us unto glory and honour.

The gospel of righteousness is revealed by faith in Christ Jesus. This is the reason why the righteous will live by faith and are also justified by faith. Therefore, we are crucified, with Christ, and we no longer live our lives the way we ought to because Christ lives in us and the life we now live is by faith in the Son of God; who loved us and gave Himself for our ransom. In Him and through our faith we may approach God with boldness and freedom. For instance, Abraham's promise came through righteousness because when God promised to make him the father of many nations, he believed God in hope, and he was not weak in faith. Abraham did not consider his body to be dead, but he staggered not at the promise of God through unbelief; but was strong in faith giving glory to God. In other words, he was persuaded by God's

"We are now crucified with Christ and we no longer live our lives the way we ought to because Christ lives in us and the life we now live is by faith in the Son of God; who loved us and gave Himself for our ransom."

promises thus, God was able to perform it and as a result, it was imputed unto him as righteous. Indeed a man is not justified by observing the law but by faith in Jesus Christ. Therefore, Christians should walk and live by faith as well as believe God.

Christians should also seek to clothe themselves in righteousness. Furthermore, they should be prepared to put on a new self, created to be like God in true righteousness and holiness. Likewise, it is also essential that Christian's pray for righteousness; walk uprightly, sow in righteousness and hunger and thirst for righteousness. This is because it is in seeking God first and His kingdom that He adds His benefits. Christians should desire to live righteously, i.e. in God's righteousness, walk in righteousness and also delight in God's righteousness. For it is by walking uprightly, sowing in righteousness, hungering and tasting after righteousness that we are truly exalted in righteousness. This is because the righteousness of God is never abolished. Also, as the scripture says righteousness exalts a nation, but sin is a disgrace for any person. Christians should strive to walk in righteousness because in it lays victory over their enemies.

It is necessary for Christians to understand that there is a blessing that comes with walking in righteousness. One of the blessings for walking in righteousness is that God's eyes are upon the righteousness, and His ears are open to their cry. This means that by walking in righteousness victory can be assured because we have the backup of God on our side. Nothing is impossible with God, and with God on our side we can overcome the kingdom of darkness contending against our destiny and evolution in Christ. God does not take His eyes off the righteous because He enthrones them as kings and exalts them forever. This also means that His eyes are upon those who fear Him and trust in His undying love. The Lord listens to the righteous when they call on him. The Bible also says that the righteous will flourish like a palm tree; they will grow like cedars of Lebanon.

> *"Nothing is impossible with God; and with God on our side we can conquer the kingdom of darkness contending against our destiny and evolution in Christ."*

The righteous will not be moved because God will judge the enemies of the righteous. God keeps the righteous, but they must be willing to fight the good fight of their faith, finish their course and keep their faith; in order to receive a crown of righteousness from God. This is the reason why wearing the breastplate of righteousness is essential and is used as a weapon of warfare because God fights for the righteous and His eyes are upon the righteousness. In other words, when they engage in any battle with the devil they are assured victory because they are walking in the Spirit and living a life of righteousness. Christian's righteousness is also linked to our total obedience to God and His instruction.

Weapon of Warfare 3- Feet for preparation of the gospel of peace

He that wins souls is wise and soul winning is essential weapon to winning against the devil schemes. God is very much interested in anyone that wins and disciple souls for His kingdom. Thus, He is ready to protect us in the day of battle. Therefore, Christians should not be ashamed of the gospel because it is the power of God for the salvation of everyone who believes: first for the Jews, then for the Gentiles. As Jesus was going about saving mankind, He expects us to do the same to the unsaved. Jesus was passionate about soul winning; so Christians must also follow His footsteps.

Wearing our helmet of salvation is indeed a weapon of warfare but more also a

> *"Wearing our helmet of salvation is indeed a weapon of warfare but more also a tool for soul winning."*

tool for soul winning. God desires His children to reach out to others by preaching the gospel of salvation to the lost. By doing so, we are able to deliver the unbelievers from the kingdom of darkness into God's marvellous light. Jesus completely saved all those who came to Him, because He always lives to intercede for them. This goes to say that not only are we required to reach out to the lost with the gospel of Christ but also to intercede for them as Jesus did for others. Christians should be prepared to produce lasting fruits, and in order to produce lasting fruits for Christ, Christians are required to be genuinely saved.

Christians should always be prepared to preach the gospel with all simplicity and boldness. Certainly, they should be willing to preach the word whether in season or out of the season. The duty of Christians is to correct the unsaved, rebuke and encourage them. We as Christians are also required to be patient with the lost and be careful in instructing them in the word. Christians should be able to reach out to the broken hearted and save those who were crushed in spirit. This is because the Lord is very close to the broken hearted, and He needs His instruments, which are Christians, to be able to save the lost.

Christian's should be prepared to open the eyes of the unsaved by turning their hearts and minds from darkness into God's marvellous light; from the power of Satan to God. This way they too will receive forgiveness of sins and a place among those who were sanctified by faith in God. Also, by so doing the eyes of the blind will be opened, and the ears of the deaf will be unstopped. As part of the preparation of the gospel of peace, Christian's should be willing to lose the bands of wickedness, and to undo the heavy burdens, and to let the oppressed go free as well as break every yoke. Likewise, they should also be willing to give their bread to the hungry, and also be ready to open their house to the poor that are cast out of their own house. If they stumble across a naked person on the street

> *"Christian's should be prepared to open the eyes of the unsaved by turning their hearts and minds from darkness into God's marvellous light; from the power of Satan to God."*

they should be prepared to clothe them and not be consumed by their own selfishness. They should steadfastly be willing to reach out to the longing soul and also satisfy the afflicted soul. This is because one of the major assignments for Christians is to be like a watered garden that reaches out to others and when they do that they automatically secure their own salvation in return. Furthermore, Christian's assignments are to build the old wasted places; to raise up the foundation of many generations. Furthermore, Christian's are called the repairers of the breaches and the restorers of the paths to dwell.

Weapon of Warfare 4 – Shield of Faith

Faith is a weapon of warfare because we need faith to have a relationship with God. In fact, faith and prayer couple together brings tremendous results. The Bible says that when praying and asking God for anything;

> *"The devil brings discouragement in the lives of Christians by attacking their hearts and minds; so that he can prevent them from activating their faith thereby avert them from getting an excellent result."*

we need to believe Him to be the rewarder of them that diligently seek him. Furthermore, we have to have faith in God for what we are asking from Him. God is willing to supply all our needs. We need to ask without wavering because those that waver are like waves in the sea that are toss to and fro by the wind, and such people should not assume that God will grant them their heart request. This is because God does not delight in double minded people because they are irregular in all their ways. Also, the devil brings discouragement in the lives of Christians by attacking their hearts and minds; so that he can prevent them from activating their faith thereby avert them from getting an excellent result. The Bible also urges believers to be transformed by renewing their mind. Do you know why? This is because anything done without faith is sin because you have doubted His ability to provide for all your needs. Christian's should be ready to be on their guard; be strong and courageous and also stand firm in their faith.

Faith is the confidence or assurance that what we hope for will happen; it gives us assurance about the things we cannot see. Faith is one of the weapons of warfare because faith helps us to believe in God and trust Him for our deliverance against our enemies. When faith is linked to prayer, results are inevitable because God answers the prayer of the righteous. God hates it when His children come to Him in disbelief because it shows that they do not trust the God they profess and that could be an insult to Him. God has

> *"Faith acts as a spiritual force that connects Christian's to God and their promise. Faith gives us victory over the works of the kingdom of darkness".*

never failed because His promises are yes and amen; He is devoted to His promise. Christians walk in fear rather than faith when wrestling with the adversary. Thus, they have given the enemy a foothold to defeat them in battle. Faith cannot be overemphasized, but it is an essential tool for Christians in their faith journey. Faith acts as a magnetic device that connects our salvation and our relationship with the Trinity. Christians are saved and justified through faith. It is impossible for Christians to live a victorious Christian life without faith. Faith acts as a spiritual force that connects Christian's to God and their promise. Faith gives us victory over the works of the kingdom of darkness. As the scriptures says: *"above all, taking the shield of faith, wherewith we are able to quench all the fiery darts of the wicked"*[62]. Faith is one of the keys of the kingdom of God because our foundation in Christ is linked to our faith and that is why without faith we cannot please God. Therefore, Christians should activate their faith by walking in faith.

Weapon of Warfare 5 – Helmet of Salvation

Wearing the helmet of salvation is ideal for the battle and without the helmet of salvation; we are likely to lose the battle against the devil. In other words, Christians should ensure that they are saved, to be able to contend against flesh and blood. The helmet of salvation is one of the armour that we have to put on. Christians need to be delivered from the power of darkness, and be translated into the kingdom of his beloved son.

God's children need to be redeemed and washed by the blood of Jesus. The Blood of Jesus cleanses us and forgive us from all our sins; thereby, giving us the power to stand and fight against flesh and blood, and against rulers of darkness, principalities, and powers. Christians should work out their own salvation with fear and trembling. This is because yesterday grace is not sufficient for today's journey. In other words, the fact that we fought and won the devil yesterday are not a perquisite that we are likely to win today's battle. Christians should be alert at all times against the devices of the devil.

Jesus Christ is indeed your salvation in times of distress. Salvation is found in no one else; for there is no other name under heaven given to men by which we must be saved. There is only one God and one mediator between God and men, by the name Christ Jesus. God has made Christians to be light for the Gentiles, that you may bring

---

[62] Ephesians 6:16 KJV

salvation to the ends of the earth. Therefore, Christians should not be ashamed of the gospel because it is the power of God for the salvation of everyone who believes: first for the Jews, then for the Gentiles. For this grace, that brings about salvation has appeared to all men. It teaches us that we should deny ungodliness and worldly lust; in order to live soberly, righteously, and godly in this present world. Christians are not genuinely saved if they fail to deny ungodliness and worldly lust. In addition to this, we are likely to fall prey to the enemies if we are still harbouring such sins. Jesus Christ gave himself for us, that He might redeem us from all iniquity, and purify unto himself a peculiar people, zealous of every good work. Thus, Christians need to walk in this same profession in order to stand against the wiles of the devil in the days of battle. Indeed salvation and glory and power belong to our God.

Christian's salvation and reputation depend on God because He is our Mighty Rock and Refuge. Indeed, God is our sun and shield; hence, no demon can be able to attack us when we are wearing our helmet of salvation. Surely, the salvation of the Lord is near those that fear Him, and we are assured victory over the devil because He is willing to save us to the uttermost those that come to Him. The Bible says that the name of the Lord is a strong tower and when the righteous run to it and they are saved. This assures us that no matter the battle we encounter or face the God that resides in us is more than able to grant us victory over our sworn enemies. It is the responsibility of Christian's, to stand firm and seek God's face. Subsequently, when we have proved to be faithful in our stewardship; then God will build a wall of fire around us in times of battle, and He will also cover our heads in days of battle.

Weapon of Warfare 6 – Sword of the Spirit

The sword of the Spirit is the word of God and Jesus Christ is the word made flesh and dwells among us. The Bible says that in the beginning was the word, and the word was with God and the word was God. Christians are to study and meditate on God's word in order to become victorious in all battles of life as well as to prosper in all their endeavours. Furthermore, we should also allow the word of God to dwell in us richly as to teach and admonish one another with all wisdom. Without the word of God dwelling in us, Christians are likely to be defeated by the devil. This is because the devil too knows the word of God to some extent. For example, he tempted Jesus when He was in the wilderness; likewise, be rest assured that he will do the same to us. Additionally, if he deceived Adam and Eve, also be rest assured that Christians are the next candidate in his agenda. Christians should be cleansed by the washing with water through the word. Also, faith can only come by hearing the word of God.

For battle to be won, Christians should be prepared to hide the word of God in the tablets of their heart. This guarantees Christians victory over their enemies. It will be impossible to capture the kingdom of darkness and forcefully take back what belongs to us without having an understanding and revelational knowledge of the word. Studying the word of God exposes Christians to their true inheritance in Christ. The word of God is so powerful that it is like fire in the bones of those who believe it. The word of God is so active that it is sharper than any two edged sword.

> *"For battle to be won; Christians should be prepared to hide the word of God in the tablets of their heart".*

There is power in the word of God and in the spoken word of God. The Bible says heaven and earth will pass away, but God's word shall not return to Him void. Besides, when we speak the word it produces results in the areas that we need change. Therefore, understanding the powers that lie in the word of God gives us a hedge and victory over the enemy.

For instance, the Bible says in God dwells all the fullness of the Godhead bodily, and we are complete in Him, who is the head of all principalities and power. Understanding the fact that we are complete in Him and God is the head of all principalities and power gives us victory over the devil

> *"There is power in the spoken word of God because it gives us a hedge and victory over the enemy."*

because we are overcomers in Christ Jesus, and the devil does not have any power over the righteous. It is essential that Christians believe God's word because there is salvation through the word. The sword of the Spirit is a weapon of warfare because it is a tool Christians use to defeat the enemy when he comes in like a flood, the spirit of the Lord (i.e. the word of God in us) will lift up a standard against him.

Weapon of warfare 7 – Prayer

Prayer is one of the keys of the kingdom of heaven because we need prayer to unlock our destiny and activate it. Christians are likely to fall prey to the schemes of the enemy without prayer. The Bible admonishes Christians to pray without ceasing. Christians should never stop praying, but rejoice in hope; be patient in tribulation, and be continuing steadfast in prayer. Once Christians are illuminated; they will undergo great and painful struggle. Christians should be prepared to persevere in the midst of trials; so that when they have done the will of God they may in return receive their promise. Christians should be ready to pray always with all prayers and supplication in the spirit. The scripture says: *"build up yourself in your most holy faith and pray in the Holy Spirit"*[63]. The Spirit of God helps our weakness. We do not know what to pray for, but the spirit itself intercedes for us with groans that words cannot be expressed. Christians should devote themselves to prayer, being watchful and thankful because the devil is extremely

---

63 Jude 1:20 KJV

subtle. As Christian's we should not be worried about anything but by prayer and petition, with thanksgiving make their request known to God. For example, Jesus Christ told His disciples to pray and never give up. Christians should be alert and on guard because we do not know when Master Jesus will return.

Prayer enables us to have access to the throne room of heaven and download coded message and mysteries from God. It is indeed a two way communication between man and God. Christians needs to dwell in the secret place of the Most High in order to abide under the shadow of the Almighty. In order to dwell in the presence of the Most High; we need to fellowship with Him. Prayer empowers and strengthens our inner man through God's spirit. It helps us to recharge our battery daily so that you do not get worn out. When we pray, we can change our world through speaking those things that are not in existence into being. When your prayer is mixed with faith, and not doubt it produces dynamic changes to any negative situation.

> *"Prayer enables us to have access to the throne room of heaven and download coded message and mysteries from God. It is indeed a two way communication between man and God".*

Prayer unlocks the doors of favour, blessing and promotion for God's children. There is some blessing, favour and promotion that will not come in the way of a Christian unless they are willing to pray like Daniel. For example, from the days of John the Baptist until now, the kingdom of heaven has been forcefully advancing, and forceful men lay hold of it. When a Christian prays, God opens the store house of heaven and pours out a blessing that their rooms are unable to contain. Christians should be prepared to fight for all that God has in store for them if they want to possess their possessions. Christians must rise and fight for what belongs to them in prayer because failure to do so will result to our fate been truncated. Prayer cannot be overemphasized because in it lays our victory over our enemies. This is because a prayerless child of God is a powerless child of God, but a prayerful child of God is a powerful child of God. Christian's frustrate the devil, when they pray, thus, he sends comforts, fake promotion and discouragement to divert the attention of God's children from praying. He preoccupies some with too many activities and materialism just to direct their attention away from God.

Prayer is a weapon of warfare because it helps us overcome every stronghold that stands on our way to the promise land. This is because God has given us authority to trample on snakes and scorpions and to overcome all the powers of the enemy; nothing will hurt us. We will also be able to pick up snakes with our hands, and when Christians drink deadly poisons; it will not hurt them at all; they will place their hands on sick people, and they

> *"Prayer is a weapon of warfare because it helps us overcome every stronghold that stands on our way to the promise land".*

will recover. This same prayer grants us victory over the enemy because we will be able to tread upon the lion and the cobra. When Christians pray the wicked are ensnared by their own transgressions of their lips and the righteous will come through trouble. When we pray, God delivers us from Satan. God promises to deliver us from every evil work and preserve us for His heavenly kingdom.

Prayer also helps in preparing us for our great assignment in God. When a Christian prays their hidden identities are revealed and exercised.

> *"Prayer unveils the mysteries that lies within the word of God and also gives you wisdom on how to exercise our authority and activate our destiny."*

Prayer unveils the mysteries that lies within the word of God and also gives us wisdom on how to exercise our authority and activate our destiny.

Prayer also teaches your hands to war as part of our preparation for our assignment. Without adequate training and our ability to understand how to rebuke the devourer; we will continuously repeat the circle. To rebuke the devourer, we need to understand ourselves and the spiritual rules of engagement because the devil is extremely subtle in his ways. His strategic plan is to deceive many into outwitting their purpose in Christ. Thus, prayer is one of the battle axe and a weapon of warfare used to prevent the devil from invading in our territory.

Weapon of Warfare 8 – Be watchful

It is essential that Christians are watchful when dealing and wrestling against the rulers of darkness of this world and principalities and powers because our adversary the devil prowls around like a roaring lion, seeking whom to devour. Christians need to be watchful so that Satan will not outsmart them with his schemes. For the end, of all things is at hand; therefore, Christians will need to be

> *"Christians need to be watchful so that Satan will not outwit them with his schemes."*

sober and watchful whilst praying. Christians should also be vigilant because they do not know what day the Lord will come. It is also essential that Christian's stay on guard and watch their territory, so that the devil will not come and obtain their blessings. The reasons why being watchful is a weapon of warfare is because Christians ought to be alert and attentive whilst praying; they should diligently watch out for their enemy.

A biblical example is the case of Nehemiah, when he was rebuilding the walls of Jerusalem. The Bible stated that he held a sword with one hand and with the other hand he continued with the rebuilding of the temple. This shows that Nehemiah and his builders were wary of their enemy so that their enemies would not outsmart them. They prepared themselves by using one hand to do the work, and the other hand to hold on to their weapons, and watch out for their enemy. In other words, Christians needs to be vigilant and watchful when they are in the battlefield. It is not enough to pray and relax because we could be attacked whilst we are relaxing. Christians can relax, but they must be quick and observant so as not to fall prey to the schemes of the devil. Christian's should be careful and cautious because they do not know when the time will come. They should always watch and pray that they may be able to escape all the wiles of the enemies and be counted worthy to stand before the Son of Man. It is also essential that they pray in the Spirit and on all occasions with all kinds of prayers and requests. They should be alert at all times and pray for all the saints. In other words, they should be prepared to commit themselves to prayer, being watchful and thankful. Even Jesus told His disciples to watch and pray so that they do not fall into temptation. Therefore, Christians should also be at alert, watch and pray so that they too will not fall prey to the devil schemes. Thus, being watchful is part of the weapon of warfare because Christians must always be on guard and watch out for their enemies.

Chapter 6 – Exercising your Authority in Christ

⚜

Christian's must understand their inheritance in Christ Jesus in order for them to exercise their authority in Christ. This is because we have not received the spirit to enslave us to fear but have received the spirit of sonship, in which we cry Abba Father. Without God, we can do nothing. He that comes to God must first believe that He is a rewarder of those that diligently seek Him. Christian's cannot exercise the authority they fail to acknowledge. For example, a person that has money in his bank account but is naive to that fact will fail to use his own money. Likewise, Christian's cannot fully maximise their full potential if they fail to recognise their true inheritance in Christ. God has given us all that pertains to life and godliness. In fact, all power and authority has He given to us in heaven and on earth. Jesus Christ has already given Christians the power and that power lies within us. As the scriptures says *"you are of God little children, and have overcome them: because greater is he that is in you, than he that is in the world"*[64].

> *"Christians cannot exercise the authority they fail to acknowledge".*

---

[64] 1 John 4:4 TBS

Understanding your Inheritance in God

The earlier Christian's acknowledges their true inheritance in Christ the better it is for them to exercise their authority over the devil. As the scripture says *"look, I have given you authority over all the power of the enemy, and you can walk among snakes and scorpions and crush them; nothing will injure you"*[65]. God has given us the power to tread upon strong lion and the cobra. Christians have the power to trample against them and when we drink or eat poisonous things we will go unscathed. Also, God has given us the power to lay hands on the sick and they shall recover. Christian's have power over evil foil, evil spirit and demonic activities; but Christian's would have to admit the fact that Jesus Christ has conquered the grave thus triumphing over the satanic kingdom. This is also why the scripture says: *"for in Him, the whole fullness of Deity (the Godhead) continues to dwell in bodily form [giving complete expression of the divine nature]. And you [f]are in Him, made full and having come to fullness of life [in Christ you too are filled with the Godhead—Father, Son and Holy Spirit—and reach full spiritual stature]. And He is the Head of all rule and authority [of every angelic principality and power].In Him also you were circumcised with a circumcision not made with hands, but in a [spiritual] circumcision [performed by] Christ by stripping off the body of the flesh (the whole corrupt, carnal nature with its passions and lusts). [Thus [g] you were circumcised when] you were buried with Him in [your] baptism, in which you were also raised with Him [[h]to a new life] through [your] faith in the working of God [[i]as displayed] when He raised Him up from the dead. And you who were dead in trespasses and in the uncircumcision of your flesh (your sensuality, your sinful carnal nature), [God] brought to life together with [Christ], having [freely] forgiven us all our transgressions, having cancelled and blotted out and wiped away the handwriting of the note (bond) with its legal decrees and demands which was in force and stood against us (hostile to us). This [note with its regulations, decrees, and*

---

65 Luke 10:19 NLT

demands] He set aside and cleared [;]completely out of our way by nailing it to [His] cross. [God] disarmed the principalities and powers that were ranged against us and made a bold display and public example of them, in triumphing over them in Him and in it [the cross]"[66]. Based on the above scripture, God dwells in all the fullness of the Godhead bodily and if He is the Godhead over principalities and power; we are therefore, complete in Him. If we are complete in God, who is the head of all principalities and powers; we are victorious over all principalities, powers, and rulers of darkness.

Another thing we need to be aware of whilst exercising our authority in Christ is that: "every God-begotten person conquers the world's ways. The conquering power that brings the world to its knees is our faith. The person who wins out over the world's ways is simply the one who believes Jesus is the Son of God"[67]. All we need to do is to believe that Jesus is the Son of God and thereby activates our faith in Christ. Until Christian's understand their inheritance in Christ and exercise their authority they will always fall prey to the victims of the kingdom of darkness. The Bible also says: "my people are destroyed for lack of knowledge"[68]. God's children are destroyed for lack the knowledge in the word of God. The word of

> *"The word of God is the key that Christian's needs to unlock their freedom, breakthrough and also activate their divine destiny".*

God is the key that Christian's needs to unlock their freedom, breakthrough and activate their divine destiny. Christian's are unable to exercise their authority in Christ because they are ignorant of their inheritance in Christ Jesus. God's children are unable to see the glorious light of the good news, because the god of this world has blinded the hearts and mind of those who do not believe. They do not understand the messages about

[66] Colossians 2: 9-15 AMP
[67] John 5:4-5 MSG
[68] Hosea 4:6 ESV

the glory of Christ who is the exact likeness of God. The devil has shifted the heart and minds of God's children from God into craving for more flamboyant and materialistic things. Christians have allowed the worries of life and the deceitfulness of wealth to choke the word of God in their hearts and soul, thereby rendering them unfruitful. As the scripture says what will it profit a man if he gains the whole world thereby loses his soul in the kingdom of God?" The devil has succeeded in using vain glory and deceitfulness of materialism to choke the word of God in the lives of Christian's; thereby, making them too busy for God's fellowship. In fact, Christian's hardly find time to study God's word because they are obsesses with acquiring more materialistic things. Christian's that are obsessed with worldly fame and recognition will find it difficult to understand their inheritance in Christ and exercise their authority.

> *"The devil has shifted the hearts and minds of God's children from God into craving for more flamboyant and materialistic things".*

God did not assure us; that the devil and the kingdom of darkness will not come after us, but He assures us that He will be with us through the fire. God also promised that anyone who attacks us must surely surrender to us. Indeed, they will conspire, lurk and watch our step just to take our life, but God promises that whosoever rages against us will be ashamed and disgraced; and those who oppose us will surely perish and come to nothing. God even assures us that: *"no weapon form against us shall prosper; and every tongue that raises up against you in judgement you will condemn. This is the heritage of the servants of the Lord, and their righteousness is of me, says the Lord"*[69]. The truth is that no one can lay anything against God's elect because it is God that justifies. Additionally, no demon has the power to condemn God's elect because

---

[69] Isaiah 54:17 KJV

Christ died, His risen and He seat at the right hand of God making intercession for us. If Christ is for us, no one can be against us because we are both risen and justified with Him through faith.

For these reasons, we can bodily say that nothing can separate us from the love of Christ. Not even our tribulation or distress, or our persecution or famine, or nakedness, or peril or sword should be able to separate us from the love of God. This counts as a test to our faith in Christ. The devil roams about seeking who he may consume by using hardships and tough times to shift Christian's focus from God. Christians

> *"The devil roams about seeking who he may consume by using hardship and tough times to shift the focus of Christian's from God".*

are a terror in the kingdom of darkness because they understand both the reasons for their existence and also their true inheritance in Christ. Jesus Christ' love has made we Christians victorious in all our tribulations and persecutions. Therefore, death, life, angel, principalities, powers, or things present, nor things to come, should not be able to separate us from the love of God; which is in Christ Jesus our Lord.

God has given us power to subdue kingdoms and cast out devil. Thus, all that Christian's need to know is to endeavour to stand their ground and exercise their authority in Christ. We have this power in Christ, because we are partakers of His inheritance and God has also delivered us from the power of darkness, and has translated us into the kingdom of His dear son. In whom we have redemption through His blood, even the forgiveness of sins. We overcame the devil by the blood and the words of our testimony. Also, having the knowledge that God created all things including dominions, principalities, and powers and being complete in Him gives us the audacity and power to cripple and disallow all the works of darkness in and around us. Indeed God is before all things, and through Him all things consist.

Christian's should endeavour to resist the devil always and then he will flee from us. In addition, God's children need to be alert and spiritually sensitive because our adversary the devil, as a roaring lion, seeks to thwart the destinies of Christian's. One more thing Christian's should also understand is that, we are seated at the right hand of the Father far above principalities and powers, and we have authority over them. Also, God is the God of more than enough and also the head of all principalities and powers. The scriptures call us gods; therefore, it is God's desires that we rule and reign as kings here on earth; to subdue all our challenges and circumstance on a daily basis because of the greater power that resides on the inside of us.

The spirit of God bears witness with our spirit, that we are the children of God, and if children, then heir; heirs of God, and joint heirs with Christ; so if we suffer with Him we will reign with Him. Christian's should also understand that the sufferings of this present time are not worthy to be compared with the glory that will be revealed in us because the earnest expectations of the creatures are waiting for the manifestation of God's children. Additionally, all things are under God's feet, and Jesus Christ is head over all things to the church. In other words, Jesus is the head over principalities and powers in the form of sickness, bondage, and captivity. This means that since Christ is the head over all things; Christian's should also be ready to dispossess the devil of their inheritance by repossessing their inheritance in Christ. Christian's should also be prepared to execute divine arrest and judgement over the devil and his kingdom; especially if they are after any department of their life such as their family and loved ones. Christians inability to exercise their legal right i.e. authority over the enemy gives him the right to torment us and our loved ones. It is also essential that Christian's, should understand that whatever they disallow in heaven is disallowed on earth and whatever they allow in heaven is allowed on earth. Besides, whatsoever we ask God in His name according to His will He promises to do it. Christian's should also resist the devil steadfastly in their faith because God assures us victory over the devil. For example, God assured us in His word that no trouble will overtake the righteous. Certainly the wicked are ensnared by the transgression of his lips, but the righteous will come through trouble. Definitely, *"the Lord will cause your enemies who rise up against you to be defeated before your face, they shall come out against you one way and flee before you seven ways"[70]*. The Lord will bring the counsels of nations to nothing and makes the plans of people of no effect. The counsel of the Lord stands forever, the plans of his heart to all generations. This is because God's angels guide, surround and deliver all those who fear Him. God has also put a hedge over us, over our households and all our possession. Undoubtedly, all the promises of God in Him are yes and in Him Amen, to the glory of God through us. God delivered us from death, and He does deliver us, in whom we trust that he will still deliver us. God also assures us that He will deliver us from every evil work and preserve us for His heavenly kingdom.

Mandates for walking in Divine Authority

The word of God is in your mouth; therefore, speak those things that are not as though they were. At the mention of the name of Jesus, every knee must bow, in heaven and on earth and under the earth. God has also assured us that every word He has uttered to us with His integrity will never be revoked.

> *"Seek the Creator and not His creation because in Him lies true riches, honour, wealth and prosperity".*

Therefore, He gives us His word to activate our inheritance in Him; and also uses it to disallow all the works of the kingdom of darkness. Also, whatsoever we decree shall be established and our light will shine in all our ways. This is the assurance

---

[70] Deuteronomy 28:7 ESV

we have in Him that if we ask Him anything according to His will He hears us. However, we need to walk in obedience to Him because if we are willing and obedient we will eat the good of the land. Be willing to seek the Creator and not His creation because in Him lies true riches, honour, wealth and prosperity.

Reigning with God

To reign with God; Christian's are to have an intimate relationship with God. Fellowshipping with God causes humanity to come into connection with divinity; thereby, actualizing their true identity in Christ. This is because only then can God reveal to us our true identity in Christ. In

> *"Fellowshipping with God causes humanity to come into connection with divinity; thereby, actualizing their true identity in Christ".*

other words, Christian's are to seek God to discover their purpose here on earth. For example, Jeremiah discovered his high calling after encountering God. Every human created under the surface of this world are destined to reign with God, but we can only reign if we are in the centre of God's will for our life. Without God's strength and enablement, Christian's cannot fulfil destiny neither can they reign in life because the devil's plan is to dispossess Christian's from their true inheritance. In order for God's children, to be victorious, over the devil's strategic plans and rule their world would require Christian's to have a right standing with God. Having a right standing with God grants us victory over our enemies.

Chapter 7 – Destined to Reign with God

D estined to reign with God is an act of the mind. As the scripture urges us *"not to copy the behaviour and the customs of this world but let God transform you into a new person by changing the way you think. Then you will learn to know God's will for you, which is good and pleasing and perfect"*[71]. Christians endeavour to serve God, by discovering their true identity in Christ. If we love the world and the things in the world our love for God is not perfected. Christian's should make up their mind to serve God despite their challenges, obstacles and misfortunes because God is prepared to turn their obstacles into testimony. However, if they faint in the days of adversity their strength is small. Also, Christian's are unstable and fearful if they do not trust God's word to come to fruition. To encounter God Christians must desire to fellowship with Him and also have faith in Him and His word. This is because without faith, it is difficult to please God. God expects us to exercise our authority in Christ during our seasons of adversity.

---

71 Romans 12:2 NLT

Mandates for Reigning with God

The oxford dictionary defines reigning as ruling and occupying the throne. God is sovereign because He rules and governs the whole world. Therefore, Christian's should be prepared to walk in God's footsteps and reign with Him. Reigning in life is a game of the mind and must be approached with adequate thought and positive confession. It is one thing to have a blue print of your desired future, and another thing to declare it and speak it into being i.e. into manifestation. The Scripture says: *"I have made you a father of many things." Abraham believed when he stood in the presence of the God who gives life to dead people and calls into existence nations that don't even exist"*[72]. There is power in positive confession because God spoke his creation into being; therefore, Christian's should also be ready to speak into being their dreams and aspirations. If God could create the heaven and earth, by calling it forth then we too must create our world by calling forth our desired outcome.

In order to reign in life; Christian's must be prepared to tackle it prayerfully. Christian's can do nothing without God. The scripture says that: "men should always pray and never give up"[73]. Also, Christian's should be determined never to stop praying. They should also be alert and sensitive at all times, and endeavour to pray in the spirit on all occasions with all kinds of prayer and requests. Jesus

> *"To be victorious in life; Christian's are required to pray without season".*

Christ was God in the form of man, but yet He prayed and tarried in God's presence all night. No wonder He ruled and reigned in this world by casting out demons, evil spirits and also setting the captives free. Jesus Christ's ability to linger in God's presence gave Him supernatural power over the devil and His cohorts. Jesus Christ was

---

[72] Romans 4:17 GWT
[73] Luke 18:1 NLT

also victorious during the day because He tarried in God's presence; likewise, Christian's are required to follow His footsteps, in order to be victorious. Christian's should stop running to men for wrong counsel because the Bible is our manual for life. To be victorious as a child of God; Christian's are to pray without season because prayer is a dialogue and a communication between God and man. Christian's should be

> *"Christian's should stop running to men for wrong counsel because the Bible is our manual for life".*

conversant with God in order to reign in life and fulfil their God's divine purpose for their life. Christians should also endeavour to have strong fellowship and intimacy with God the Father, God the Son and God the Holy Spirit.

To rule and dominate your world as a Christian will require you to discover your purpose in Christ. This is because God created all things such as the heaven, earth, visible and invisible, whether thrones, or dominions, or principalities or even powers. God created all things by Himself and for Himself and He is before all things because in Him all things consist. Therefore, if God is the originator of your purpose and you are obedient to Him and His precepts you are guaranteed to rule and reign in life. God has made provisions for His vision and assignment in your life. The scripture says: "my God will liberally supply ([a]fill to the full) your every need according to His riches in glory in Christ Jesus."[74] Also, the scripture also says that "God's divine power has given us everything we need for life and for godliness. This power was given to us through knowledge of the one who called us by his own glory and integrity"[75]. The blessings and provision of God in one's life is what causes one to reign in life, and His blessings makes rich and adds no sorrow. This is because in God lies true riches, honour,

---

74 Philippians 4:19 AMP
75 2 Peter 1:3 GWT

wealth and prosperity. Once a Christian is in the centre of God's will for his life, his needs are met. This is because God is the best employer of a man because His pay check is better than what any man can give. Also, God assures us of both earthly and heavenly currencies. A Christian is also likely to make

"God is the best employer of a man because in Him you are guaranteed of both earthly and heavenly currencies".

tremendous impact in the lives of others when his in the centre of God's will for his life. It is when we are fulfilling destiny that nations celebrate us. For instance, it was when Jesus was at the centre of the will of God for His life that fame located Him. Jesus Christ impacted

"Beware of good gifts from men because the devil uses good gifts to ensnare Christian's from fulfilling destiny".

the lives of others because He was walking in His divine purpose. The devil is ready to ensnare Christian's in order to prevent them from fulfilling their divine

destiny. This is the reason why some Christian's have forfeited their divine destiny by indulging in their own self will. Beware of good gifts from men because the devil uses good gifts to ensnare Christian's from fulfilling destiny. Brethren, not all that glisters are gold; so we need to be alert and wary of the devil devices.

In order to reign with God, and fulfil destiny Christian's are require to undergo some adversity. So many people call it different names such as the school of thought, whilst others call it prison gate; for others, it is called periods of uncertainties, whilst some refer to it as wilderness experience and others darkest night. It is up to us to call it whatever we like, but these seasons of adversity

"God uses our seasons of uncertainties and adversity to prepare us for our divine assignment".

are design by God, to educate us and prepare us for our great assignment in God. The scripture says: *"if we endure hardship, we will reign with*

Him. If we deny Him, He will deny us[76]. It is necessary to note that if we disown Him before men; He will also disown us before His Father in heaven. If we share His sufferings, we will also share His glory.

"For if, by the trespass of the one man, death reigned through that one man, how much more will those who receive God's abundant provision of grace and of the gift of righteousness reign in life through the one man, Jesus Christ"[77]. God is ready to confer unto us His kingdom just as His Father conferred it to Him. His plan for us is to judge all things and dine with Him in His kingdom. Seeking other alternatives in the expense of God's will deprive us of receiving our crown of glory. In order to receive this crown of glory we need to be faithful to the end. Christian's should not allow impatience to rob them from their blessing and inheritance in Christ. If we say that the Lord delays at His coming and we seek other alternative; when the Bridegroom shall come He will appoint to us a portion with the unbelievers. Certainly, the season of adversity could be draining and demanding, but it acts as an avenue that God uses to perfect our calling in Christ. God desires to humble, prune and equip us for our future glory.

Things to avoid – Hindrances to Reigning with God

It is one thing to discover purpose and it is another thing to walk in the line of purpose. When chance and adequate preparation meet success is inevitable. Likewise, divine purpose is actualized. The fact that we have discovered purpose does not guarantee our likelihood of fulfilling our purpose. Do not bury your talents and purpose in

> *"When chance and adequate preparation meet success is inevitable. Likewise, divine purpose is actualized. The fact that we have discovered purpose does not guarantee our likelihood of fulfilling our purpose."*

[76] 2 Timothy 2:12 NLT
[77] Romans 5:17 NIV

the grave. There is a saying that a lot of great potential and talents are buried in the grave. This is because many discovered purpose but failed to fulfil it hence allowed the purpose of God within them to die dormant. Others have wasted the oil that was poured on them because they were running after the cares of the world. Do not allow the grace of God within you to lie dormant because nations are waiting for your manifestation and you could be the miracle in someone else's life. Therefore, in order to reign in life; we need to be determined to pay whatsoever price our destiny (purpose) in God might cost us.

Reigning with God is a process and the processes are determined by our expected outcome and how well we learn our lessons of adversity. Christian's are required to have faith in God; believe in themselves and their visions, in order, to get to their expected end. Christian's should avoid the distractions of the world and the world's definitions of success. This is because the world defines success as having in possessions materialistic achievements but God's definitions defers. God's success is not defined by the world's popularity. Biblically, following God requires Christian's to deny themselves of all their earthly possessions. For example, Apostle Paul counted all things as loss for the sake of Christ; in order to know Him, and the power of His resurrection, and fellowship of His sufferings, being made conformable unto His death.

Christian's cannot serve both God and mammon because we are either for Christ or against Him. This is the reason why Christian's are to give up everything in order to become God's disciples (followers). Christian's are likely to have divided attention when they fail to discard all for God. This is because it is impossible to serve both God and mammon. Indeed, no one can serve two masters at the same time. For example, in the case of a rich man, Jesus asked him to sell his whole belongings and give to the poor; the Bible recorded that the rich man went away sorrowful because he had vast possessions. Jesus told him that in order to receive eternal life *"go and sell your possession and give to the poor, and you will have treasures in heaven. Then come, follow me"*[78]. The rich man was unwilling to pay his price required for his eternal life. God's reply was that; it is difficult for a rich man to enter the kingdom of heaven. This is because whosoever is bent on saving his mundane life, his comfort, and security here on earth shall lose his eternal life; and whoever loses his life, his comfort and security here on earth for God's sake shall have an everlasting life. *For what will it profit a man if he gains the whole world and forfeits his life [his blessed [q]life in the kingdom of God]? Or what would a man give as an exchange for his [blessed] [r]life [in the kingdom of God]*[79]?

God defines success as being in the centre of His divine will, plan and purpose. When Christian's seek God, He makes provisions for all their needs. The world is bent on seeking the gift rather than the giver of the gift which is Jesus Christ. Christian's have missed it in the process of seeking God's benefits. God should always be our number one priority if we want to arrive safely to our destination. It is God's intension for us all to reign in life, but we must follow His principles and footsteps in order to get to His expected end for our lives. It is indeed a gradual process that requires our total obedience and surrender to God. Christian's should endeavour to have faith, patience, fruits of the spirit, zeal and passion for God's word because these are the requirements of fulfilling God's divine providence.

Words of Encouragement

Therefore, I cease this opportunity to encourage Christian's not to allow fear to deprive them of fulfilling God's divine destiny because nations are waiting for their manifestation. God delights in showing

---

[78] Matthew 19:21; Mark 10:17-22 AMP
[79] Matthew 16:25-26; Mark 8:36 AMP

forth His glory and personality through us but we have to learn how to believe in Him and trust Him even when we cannot trace Him. The only hindrances of becoming the salt of the earth, the light of the world and a city set on a hill that cannot be hidden are by allowing fear to cripple and paralyze our belief system. Fear indeed has torment and is a killer of divine destiny. Satan uses fear to camouflage Christian's divine destiny. Fear is also an enemy of God and also of our divine destination because it thwarts God's children from freely possessing all that God has in store for them. Fear prevents God's children from stepping out of the known into the unknown; where the blessings of God await them. It also cripples Christian's ability to step out of faith into God's predestined glory and future. This fear must be captured and dealt with; in order to fulfil our mandate and high calling in God.

Therefore, be determined to capture this fear that wants to erode us from actualizing this magnificent destiny in God. Christian's should also be ready and determined to affect humanity because nations are waiting for their manifestation. Furthermore, their ability to affect humanity will forever leave a legacy as one of God's generals who made history by touching the lives of many.

God bless you.